The Modern Losing Trick Count

Accurate bidding is the key to success at the bridge table, and the secret of good bidding lies in evaluating your cards in a sensible way. It is not just a matter of adding up the high-card points, for the point-count does not always tell the whole story. To achieve consistent bidding accuracy you have to do what the experts do – count losers.

The Losing Trick Count is a tried and trusted method of hand evaluation which has stood the test of time. Ron Klinger, famous Australian author who has more good books to his credit than many players have good hands, has brought the LTC up to date by relating it to modern systems and conventions.

You cannot fail to benefit from a study of this remarkably simple method. The Losing Trick Count can be applied within the parameters of any bidding system, and it is effective even if your partner has never heard of the method. It will enable you to bid those 20-point games and distributional slams that previously seemed beyond reach. The result will be more hits and fewer misses, and this is bound to increase both the profit and the pleasure which you derive from the game.

'It updates the methods for valuing hands written by Courtenay and Walshe in 1935. Consciously, or sub-consciously, this is the way experts decide whether or not to bid games and slams. It is well worth the money.'

– Derek Rimington, Jersey Evening Post

by Ron Klinger

The Modern Losing Trick Count

Bidding to Win at Bridge

by

RON KLINGER

with a Foreword by Hugh Kelsey

LONDON

VICTOR GOLLANCZ LTD

in association with Peter Crawley

1989

First published in Great Britain in February 1987
in association with Peter Crawley
by Victor Gollancz Ltd
14 Henrietta Street, London WC2E 8QJ
Second impression April 1989

To Ben and Viv

British Library Cataloguing in Publication Data
Klinger, Ron
    Modern losing trick count : bidding to win
    at bridge—(Master bridge series)
    1. Contract bridge—Bidding
    I. Title   II. Series
    795.41'52   GV1282.4

    ISBN 0–575–03973–6

Photoset and printed in Great Britain by
WBC Print Ltd, Bristol

Contents

Foreword

by Hugh Kelsey

In my own writings I have tended to concentrate on the finer points of play and defence, aspects of the game that hold an endless fascination for me. But in my heart of hearts I have to acknowledge that the bidding is roughly three times as important as the play. In the upper reaches of the game standards are such that there is little to choose between the contestants in the matter of card play. At lower levels the picture is the same. It is accurate bidding that wins the matches, the tournaments and the rubbers. If you can consistently reach sensible contracts, you will have few problems in the play of the cards.

The Losing Trick Count is a method of hand evaluation that has been around for a long time – almost as long as the game itself. One of my treasured possessions is a copy of the first book on the subject: *The Losing Trick Count* by Courtenay and Walshe, published in 1935. All experts make use of this method either knowingly or subconsciously, and yet the LTC has never achieved wide popularity with the mass of players who remain wedded to the point-count for evaluating their hands.

The point-count is all very well in its way, but it is an inflexible method of valuation even if points are added for length or shortage according to the dictates of the preferred authority. While accurate enough for the purposes of no-trump play, the point-count becomes woefully inadequate when a good trump fit has been found. After missing an excellent distributional game, partners will often shrug their shoulders and tell each other: 'We couldn't bid it; we had only 20 points.' This is a sad commentary on the average standard of bidding.

In this book the renowned Australian player/writer, Ron Klinger, reveals the secrets of bidding 20 point games and 25-point slams. You have to count your *losers* to achieve a proper estimate of the trick-taking potential of the hands. The Losing Trick Count is brought up to date and the reader is shown how it can be applied simply and efficiently to every aspect of modern bidding.

The method is not intended to replace the point-count but to supplement it. And it makes not the slightest difference which system of bidding you favour. The LTC can be applied within the context of any system, and it is guaranteed to give you that slight edge that makes the difference between winning and losing.

On reading this book I was impressed once again by the timeless nature of accurate hand evaluation. The methods that were sound fifty years ago are just as valid today. The author has related the LTC to many modern conventions, some of which will be unfamiliar to a number of players, but all are worth while and a little study will be repaid a thousand-fold.

The most fascinating aspect of the Losing Trick Count is that it can be applied with profit even if your partner has never heard of the method. Acting on your own, you can improve your bidding results by at least 20%. Naturally, if your partner is on the same wavelength the gain is compounded.

Now, for entertainment and profit, I pass you over to Ron Klinger. Read, absorb and enjoy!

1

There is a Better Way

Introduction to the Losing Trick Count

To start, try this little test. You pick up:

♠ K 10 8 6 4 3　♡ 7　◇ 4 3　♣ A 8 4 2

Partner opens 1 Diamond. You respond 1 Spade. Partner rebids with 4 Spades. What action do you take?

If you are among the vast majority of bridge players, you will choose to pass 4 Spades. Perhaps you pass because you take 4 Spades to be a shut out bid. Perhaps you recognise that partner has made a strong bid, but so what? After all, you have only seven points or so, maybe a bit extra for the singleton. Right?

Wrong! When the lead is made and you see dummy, you notice, with a familiar sinking feeling, that you should be in slam. The complete hand is:

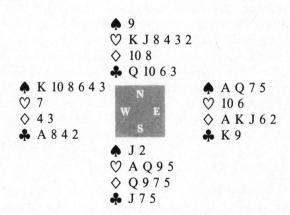

```
                    ♠ 9
                    ♡ K J 8 4 3 2
                    ◇ 10 8
                    ♣ Q 10 6 3
♠ K 10 8 6 4 3              N        ♠ A Q 7 5
♡ 7                   W         E    ♡ 10 6
◇ 4 3                      S         ◇ A K J 6 2
♣ A 8 4 2                           ♣ K 9
                    ♠ J 2
                    ♡ A Q 9 5
                    ◇ Q 9 7 5
                    ♣ J 7 5
```

You ruff the second heart, draw trumps in two rounds and ruff your club losers in dummy, not too tough a play. Without a heart lead you would aim to establish the diamond suit to discard the heart loser. Still, twelve tricks were easy.

Partner looks at you, you look at partner. Partner asks "Could we have bid six?" "No," you reply, despite an uneasy feeling. "We had only 24 points."

At rubber, you might dismiss it as just another fluke result. At duplicate, you open the scoresheet and find that your result is under average. Most pairs are 4 Spades like you but some have made seven and one or two pairs are in 6 Spades, scoring the slam. You dismiss them imperiously, "Probably didn't know what they were doing."

Chances are, however, that they knew exactly what they were doing. They were able to assess the value of the two hands more accurately than the vast majority of bridge players whose horizons are limited by counting points, even though they may add and subtract points for half a dozen or more factors.

If you are content to plod along as you have been in the past and accept the regular 2♡-making-four, 4♠-making-six results, read no further. If, on the other hand, you would like to be able to bid the 21-point games, the 24-point slams, the way the experts do, this book is going to be ideal for you. It is written, not for the world class player, but for the ninety-odd per cent of players who fail to extract the full value of their cards, who do not attain what is rightfully theirs. Well before the end of the book, you will consider the above slam child's play, as you bid your thin games and slams with confidence and stay out of the superficially attractive games or slams which are poor odds to succeed.

Although some of the areas covered will be familiar to experts, there may also be some ideas from which even they can benefit. Judging by the actual results in the world championships, the experts still have a lot to learn about slam bidding.

What is the losing trick count?

Why do we count points? Purely as a guide to the number of tricks we figure to win. 26 points means a game is probable, 33 points and a slam is likely. The **Losing Trick Count** (called the **LTC** from here on) is a different means of assessing the number of tricks the partnership is likely to win. It is used after a trump fit has been established and is clearly superior to counting points because more accurate assessments are obtained more often.

Suppose you pick up, lucky you:

♠ A   ♡ 7   ◇ A K Q 9 8 7 6 4 3 2   ♣ 6

What is your hand worth?

If you thought of this as thirteen points, even for a fleeting moment, your bridge concepts require a drastic overhaul. The hand should be viewed as 11 winners, 2 losers, and all you need to know is whether partner can cover both your losers, only one of them or none at all. The Blackwood Convention, sooner or later, will solve this problem.

The **LTC** operates in a similar way, even though your winners and losers are nowhere near as clearcut as in the above example. The **LTC** enables you to gauge the playing strength of your own hand and estimate accurately the trick-taking potential of your partner's hand. Put both of these assessments together and you can tell the number of tricks the partnership will win most of the time.

Sounds easy? You will be surprised just how easy it all is.

The Losing Trick Count appeared originally in 1935 in a book entitled *The Losing Trick Count* by F. Dudley Courtenay and Col. G. G. J. Walshe. It was given scant attention then (despite the subtitle "*As used by the leading Contract Bridge Tournament Players, with examples of Expert Bidding and Expert Play*") and came to light again in 1961 through the endeavours of Maurice Harrison-Gray who brought out a brief pamphlet again titled *The Losing Trick Count*. The **LTC** first came to my attention in Jeff Ruben's brilliant work *The Secrets Of Winning Bridge* (1969) and since then it has made brief appearances in other works such as Albert Dormer's *Powerhouse Hands* (1975), Robert D. Sundby's *Bridge in the '80s* (1984), my own *Cue Bidding To Slams* (1983) and a number of books authored by George Rosenkranz: *The Romex System of Bidding* (1970), *Win With Romex* (1975), *Bid Your Way To The Top* (1978), *Bridge, The Bidder's Game* (1985) and, in conjunction with Alan Truscott, *Modern Ideas In Bidding* (1982). In 1984, a very brief summary entitled *The Losing Trick Count* by D. C. Griffiths appeared in the Bridge Player's Handbook Series, published by Probay Press Ltd. In many of these works, the treatment accorded to the **LTC** was no more than cursory and it is time to give due recognition to the extent and usefulness of this method.

The **LTC** made little impression on me in the early 1970s since I was so raw but it did not take long to become dissatisfied with the traditional hand-valuation techniques. Most were inefficient – you simply failed to reach the correct contracts on too many occasions. Those methods that enjoyed a higher rate of success were just too cumbersome – you needed a computer or unlimited time to make the never-ending calculations.

What was needed was a method that was highly efficient and easy to calculate. After years of experimentation and analysis, I believe the *Modern Losing Trick Count* is bound to improve your bidding skills. You will bid more accurately and also more confidently. Best of all you will win more often. Even though you may be sceptical right now, you will surprise yourself on the first few occasions that the **LTC** gives you a great result, one that you would have missed using your old methods. Once these results start coming regularly, not only will you be on the victory dais more often but you will also be having much more fun.

By the end of the book you will have no trouble reaching 4♠ on 20 hcp:

WEST	EAST
♠ A Q 8 7 6	♠ K 9 5 2
♡ 7 3	♡ 8 6 4 2
◇ A Q J 4 2	◇ 7 6
♣ 6	♣ A 9 3

or avoiding problems by stopping in a comfortable 2♠ on 24 hcp on:

WEST	EAST
♠ A Q 8 7 6	♠ K 9 5 2
♡ 9 7 3	♡ J 8 6
◇ A Q J	◇ K 7 6
♣ 6 5	♣ K J 4

or finding immaculate grand slams such as this 7♠ with just 27 hcp:

WEST	EAST
♠ A 8 7 6 2	♠ K Q 5 4 3
♡ A K 8 6 3	♡ 7 2
◇ 9	◇ A K 6
♣ 7 2	♣ A 9 5

Enough of this tantalizing. Stop drooling over that grand slam and let's get to work.

2

The Basic Losing Trick Count

How To Assess The Partnership's Playing Strength

The **LTC** can be used *after a trump fit has been established*. It is not designed for no trump hands and is quite unsuitable for misfit hands. Thus, it is vital that you do not envisage the **LTC** as replacing point count. It is used as an adjunct to the point count when a trump fit comes to light. *After the trump fit is known*, the **LTC** will give a more accurate guide to the potential of the partnership hands.

The LTC formula:

1. **Count**   *Your losers*
2. **Add**   *Partner's losers*
3. **Deduct**   *This total from 24*

The answer is the number of tricks the partnership can expect to win.

The **LTC** does not guarantee that you will in fact make this number of tricks. Do not expect your insurance company to underwrite your contract on the basis of the **LTC** potential.

The **LTC** answer is the number of tricks you can expect to win *if suits break normally and half of your finesses work*. In other words, it is the number of tricks that will be won *most of the time*. If three out of three finesses fail, or if trumps break 4–0, it would be unreasonable to blame the **LTC** for your wretched luck.

The calculations are not complicated since there are only two stages:

1. *Counting your losers*
2. *Assessing partner's losers*

You will not experience difficulty with either of these aspects and we examine each in turn:

Counting Your Losers

The Raw Count

Count losers only in the first three cards of each suit.
(The 4th, 5th, 6th etc. cards in a suit are taken as winners.)
With three or more cards in a suit:
Count the A, K and Q as winners; anything lower is a loser.
With two cards in a suit:
Count the A and K as winners; anything lower is a loser.
With one card in a suit:
Count the A as a winner; anything lower is a loser.
There are never more than three losers in a suit. There are never more losers in a suit than the number of cards in the suit.

Examples

Holding	Losers	Holding	Losers	Holding	Losers
J 10 9	3	8 7 6 4	3	10 9 6 5 3 2	3
A 6 4	2	A 6 4 3	2	A 6 4 3 2	2
K 8 3	2	Q J 10 2	2	K J 6	2
K Q 6	1	K Q 8 6	1	K Q 8 6 5	1
A K 9	1	A Q 7 3	1	A Q 8 6 4 3	1
A K Q	0	A K Q 7 2	0	A K Q 8 6 5 4	0
J 3	2	Q 6	2	Q J	2
A 6	1	K	1	K Q	1
A K	0	A	0	Void	0

Axiom 1: As points increase, losers decrease; as points decrease, losers increase:

♠ A K 6 4	=	1 loser
♡ K Q 9 3	=	1 loser
◇ J 3	=	2 losers
♣ 4 3 2	=	3 losers
13 points	:	7 losers

♠ A K 6 4	=	1 loser
♡ K Q 9 3	=	1 loser
◇ A 9	=	1 loser
♣ 4 3 2	=	3 losers
16 points	:	6 losers

♠ A K 6 4	=	1 loser
♡ K Q 9 3	=	1 loser
◇ A 9	=	1 loser
♣ K 3 2	=	2 losers
19 points	:	5 losers

♠ A K 6 4	=	1 loser
♡ K Q 9 3	=	1 loser
◇ A K	=	0 losers
♣ K 3 2	=	2 losers
22 points	:	4 losers

Axiom 2: The more balanced a hand, the more losers; the more unbalanced a hand, the fewer the losers:

♠ A K 6 4	=	1 loser	♠ A K 6 4 2	=	1 loser
♡ K Q 9 3	=	1 loser	♡ K Q 9 3	=	1 loser
◇ J 3	=	2 losers	◇ J 3	=	2 losers
♣ 4 3 2	=	3 losers	♣ 4 2	=	2 losers
13 points	:	7 losers	13 points	:	6 losers

♠ A K 6 4 2	=	1 loser	♠ A K 6 5 4 2	=	1 loser
♡ K Q 9 3 2	=	1 loser	♡ K Q 9 3 2	=	1 loser
◇ J 3	=	2 losers	◇ J 3	=	2 losers
♣ 4	=	1 loser	♣ —	=	0 losers
13 points	:	5 losers	13 points	:	4 losers

Even if self-evident, these fundamental principles are worth repeating:

As the points increase, the losers decrease.
As the points decrease, the losers increase.
The more unbalanced the hand, the fewer the losers.
The more balanced the hand, the more losers.

Let's take another look at the slam hand from the previous chapter (see page 1), using just the Raw **LTC** Count:

	You		*Dummy*	
2 losers	♠ K 10 8 6 4 3		♠ A Q 7 5	1 loser
1 loser	♡ 7		♡ 10 6	2 losers
2 losers	◇ 4 3		◇ A K J 6 2	1 loser
2 losers	♣ A 8 4 2		♣ K 9	1 loser
7 losers				5 losers

Your losers	:	7	Deduct from 24 = 12, the
Add partner's losers	:	5	number of tricks expected if
Total losers	:	12	spades are trumps (and the breaks are normal).

Your partnership should reach 6 Spades. A sensible auction would be:

You	Partner	
	1 ◇	
1 ♠	4 ♠	
4NT	5 ♡	
6 ♠	Pass	

Note incidentally that there is nothing special or unusual about opener's hand – no voids, no singletons, no freak fit. If anything, it is slightly light for the jump to 4 Spades.

Counting the Queen as a Winner

It clearly cannot be correct to value a queen as highly as an ace. Obviously Q-7-3 is not nearly as powerful as A-7-3. Just as obviously, Q-7-3 is more valuable than 8-7-3, so that it is better than three losers.

The queen should be counted as a full value, a winner, whenever it is supported by another honour. If the queen has only rags with it, Q-9-8 or worse, count it as only half a trick, and thus as $2\frac{1}{2}$ losers.

Therefore, A-K-Q = no losers, A-Q-6 = 1 loser, K-Q-3 = 1 loser, Q-J-5 = 2 losers and Q-10-7 = 2 losers BUT Q-8-3 = $2\frac{1}{2}$ losers, Q-7-5-4 = $2\frac{1}{2}$ losers, Q-9-6-5-2 = $2\frac{1}{2}$ losers, and so on.

The value of "togetherness" for bridge honours in well-known:

(a)	Dummy	:	K Q 6		(b)	Dummy	:	K 7 6
	Declarer	:	7 5 4			Declarer	:	Q 5 4

In (a), you have a 50% chance of two tricks. In (b), the chance for two tricks (lead low to one honour, duck on the way back) is a measly 19%, unless the opponents kindly lead the ace for you. (The chance of two tricks for (b) improves as you hold more cards in the two hands, but (a) always has a higher trick potential until you have 11 cards together).

(c)	Q J 6		(d)	Q 6 4
	4 3 2			J 3 2

With (c), you have a 75% chance of one trick (lead twice towards dummy); in (d) the chance for a trick is a shade above 30% (unless they lead the suit for you).

(e)	Q 10 3		(f)	Q 6 3
	6 5 4			10 5 4

With (e), the chance for one trick is $37\frac{1}{2}$% (lead towards dummy, finessing the 10 if second hand plays low; if this draws the A or K, later lead towards the Q). In (f) the chance for a trick is barely above 25%.

Even if partner has bid the suit, Q-x-x or Q-x-x-x may be no more than a moderate holding. High level contracts where the trump suit is:

	OR	
Q 6 5		Q 7 4 2
opposite		opposite
K 8 4 3 2		A 6 5 3

are no great delight.

Examples of counting losers involving the queen:

♠ K Q 7	=	1 loser		♠ Q 6 5 2	=	2½ losers
♡ A Q 8 5 3	=	1 loser		♡ Q J 8 3	=	2 losers
◊ Q 7 2	=	2½ losers		◊ A 7 6	=	2 losers
♣ 7 3	=	2 losers		♣ Q 4	=	2 losers*
		6½ losers				8½ losers

*Note that with a doubleton, any card below the A and K is a loser, so that Q-x is two losers, not 1½.

Assessing Partner's Losers

On the surface this seems to be a tough problem but in reality it is no more difficult than gauging partner's points. If you can tell how strong partner's hand is, you can calculate the losers. The basis is:

Minimum Opening Hand = 7 losers

We have seen that the actual losers vary according to strength and shape. Nevertheless, the average minimum opening is around the 7 loser mark and this is the best starting point for your assessment. These are routine 1 Club openings on around 13 points:

♠ A Q 7 4		♠ 7 6 4
♡ J 4		♡ K 3
◊ 6 3 2		◊ 9 8 3
♣ A K 9 3		♣ A K Q 8 6

Note that each hand has 7 losers.

You calculate partner's losers based on the strength revealed in the bidding.

A simple working guide would look like this:

Points	Description of Strength		Expectancy
13-15	Sound Minimum Opening	=	6-7 losers
16-18	Strong Opening	=	5-6 losers
19-21	Very Strong Opening	=	4-5 losers
22-up	Game Force Opening	=	3 losers or fewer
10-12	Just Below Normal Opening	=	8 losers
7-9	Well Below Sound Opening	=	9 losers

Accordingly, if the bidding begins:

Partner	You
1♣	1♡
2♡ ...	

partner has shown a minimum opening and you should expect 7 losers.

Had the bidding started:

Partner	You
1♣	1♡
3♡	

partner would be showing a stronger hand. As partner is bidding for one trick more, you are entitled to expect one loser less. The normal holding for the sequence is 6 losers.

If the bidding began:

Partner	You
1♢	1♠
4♠ ...	

partner would be showing a very strong hand. As a minimum rebid would be 2♠, partner's jump to 4♠ is two tricks extra, and so should hold two losers less. The normal holding for this sequence would be 5 losers.

We can now see how you would go about assessing the hand with which we started chapter 1:

♠ K 10 8 6 4 3   ♡ 7   ♢ 4 3   ♣ A 8 4 2

Partner opens 1 Diamond, you respond 1 Spade and partner's rebid is 4 Spades. What now?

Your thoughts would speed swiftly along these lines: "We have a good trump fit. I hold 7 losers. Partner has shown two tricks better than a minimum opening and so should have 5 losers. $7+5=12$. $24-12=12$. I see we have potential here for a slam. I must therefore keep on bidding and must not pass it out at 4 Spades."

How you keep on bidding will depend on your partnership's slam techniques. Here Blackwood 4NT is a sensible move but on other hands cue bidding might be the right approach (but only if the partnership is familiar with cue bidding techniques, of course).

(Incidentally, that sequence – 1♢ : 1♠, 4♠ – is *not* a "shut out" by opener. Shut out bids occur only on the first round of bidding and are designed to keep the opponents out of the auction. There is no such concept as a shut out with opener's rebid. The reason is that if the bidding has been, say, 1♢ : 1♠ : (Pass), whom would opener want to shut out? Two opponents who could not enter the auction on the first round?

Some confuse the given auction with 1♠ : 4♠, where the 4♠ response is a shut out, but that *does* occur on the first round of bidding and is designed to keep fourth player out of the bidding. Opener's rebid is based on the value of the hand, not on pre-emptive principles. Opener's 4♠ rebid can be termed a "sign off" since from opener's point of view, 4♠ is the limit of the hand opposite the minimum of six points promised by responder. However, it is a conditional sign off, and responder is entitled to bid on with sufficient extra values.

Loser expectancy for various actions :

These will be examined in greater detail in later chapters but you should already be able to calculate the minimum losers expected for the following actions.

How many losers would you expect in partner's hand for these bids :

(a)   1NT opening, strong, 16–18 points

(b)   1NT opening, Precision, 13–15 points

(c)   Takeout double by an unpassed hand

(d)   Jump-raise, forcing to game, 13 points or more, e.g. 1♡ : 3♡

(e)   Jump-rebid by opener in own suit, e.g. 1♣ : 1♠, 3♣

Answers

(a)   6 losers. Better than a minimum opening.

(b)   7 losers. Minimum opening.

(c)   7 losers or better. Expectancy for the double is opening values.

(d)   7 losers or better, since the bid is based on 13 points or more.

(e)   5-6 losers. The bid shows a better than minimum opening, usually around the 15-17 point mark with a six-card suit. A hand of 4 losers would definitely be too strong for this action, and with a 4-loser single-suited minor hand, opener should choose either a different opening or a different rebid, depending on what is available in the partnership's system.

How Does It All Operate?

1. Why deduct the losers from 24?

What are the most losers you are permitted to count in one suit? Answer : Three. therefore, how many losers maximum could you have in your whole hand? Answer : Twelve. So, what is the maximum number of losers in your hand plus partner's hand? Answer : 24.

The **LTC** operates by deducting the actual losers from the maximum possible total. What accounts for this difference? Why are you not losing more? *Because of the tricks you are going to win.* It would be feasible to count winners instead of losers, but this would be a longer mental process since one would have to count every card beyond the fourth as a winner. It could be done but the **LTC** does it more quickly. The simplest way of looking at it is :

Maximum possible losers (24) – Actual losers = Tricks expected.

Some texts (Harrison-Gray, Griffiths) recommend that you deduct the losers from 18 and the answer then indicates the level to which you should bid. This is quite all right since all that is happening when you deduct the partnership's losers from 18 is that you have already deducted the "book" of six tricks from the maximum possible losers, 24.

Nevertheless, my strong preference is to encourage players to work from 24 since this relates directly to the losers and the trick-taking capacity, which is what the **LTC** is all about. Using 24 as the base for deduction also demystifies the process and the ultimate answer is in terms of tricks expected to be won. This gives players a better grasp of hand valuation and translating tricks expected into contract to be bid is not too daunting a task.

2. How good must the trump fit be?

At this early stage, you can utilise the **LTC** whenever you have a decent 8-card or longer trump fit. Later we will see that adjustments should be made for excellent trump fits ("super-fits") for which we should deduct a loser or for poor trump combinations for which we should add a loser.

The **LTC** operates soundly on the basis of a 9-card trump fit or a good 8-card fit, such as the 4-4 fit. With lesser 8-card fits, such as the 5-3 or 6-2, you should add a loser unless the 3-card or doubleton support is excellent (J-10-x / Q-x-x or better, or J-10 / Q-x or better).

3. How can you rely on the fourth card in a suit as a winner?

Take this situation :

♠ K 9 8 3
♡ 7 4
◇ K J 7 2
♣ 6 5 3

Partner opens 1 Club, you bid 1 Spade and partner replies 3 Spades. What would you do?

You count your hand as 9 losers and partner should have 6 losers (one less than the 7 losers that would be shown by a minimum raise to 2 Spades). $9 + 6 = 15 \ldots 24 - 15 = 9$. Tricks expected $= 9$. Therefore, pass 3 ♠.

Why is the fourth spade not a loser? Because partner will have four spades to raise your suit and with the normal 3-2 break, the fourth round will be a winner.

What about the fourth diamond? If partner happened to have four diamonds, the normal 3-2 break will provide a fourth-round winner. In the more likely case that partner has less than four diamonds, the fourth can be trumped in partner's hand. In other words, if the fourth or fifth round of a non-trump suit is not already a winner, it will usually be possible to eliminate these losers by ruffing them in partner's hands, since the **LTC** operates only when a sound trump fit is held.

4. How can you count holdings like A-Q-x or K-Q-x as one loser, two winners? Isn't this overvaluing your cards?

In the play it is easy to calculate the trick-taking potential of card combinations :

(a) Dummy : A Q 6

Declarer : 7 4 3

(b) Dummy : K Q 5

Declarer : 6 4 2

The chance for two tricks in each case is 50%, depending on the key missing card being on declarer's left.

In the bidding, however, you do not know partner's exact holding. Nevertheless, the potential of these holdings to produce two tricks is excellent, far greater than 50%.

For example, take a look at the A-Q-x holding. There are three positions for the critical missing card, the king :

K 4 3

 K 4 3   K 4 3

You : A Q 6   *You :* A Q 6   *You :* A Q 6

If the king is on your right, you have two tricks. If the king is with your partner, your A-Q is worth two tricks. Only when the king is on your left would you lose two tricks. Hence two tricks will be won at least two times out of three, and the chance of two tricks is at least 66⅔%.

However, if you and your partner are the ones bidding, who is more likely to hold the king, partner or the opposition? If partner has indicated strength in the auction, it is 50-50 whether partner has the critical king or an opponent has it. For instance, suppose you hold 14 points and partner's bidding reveals a 13-point hand. As partner has 50% of the missing points, partner has a 50% chance of holding the key king. In such a case, the chance for two tricks for your A-Q-x increases to 75% – 50% of the time partner has it and half of the rest of the time it will be on your right. The more points held by partner, the more likely it will be that the missing king is there and not with an opponent.

Add to this the other incidental chances such as partner's holding

J-x-x (making two tricks a certainty) or 10-9-x (making two tricks about a 75% chance) or a lead into the A-Q-x, and the chances for two tricks with this holding rise to over 80%.

Precisely the same reasoning makes K-Q-x likely to produce two tricks a high percentage of the time : if the ace is with partner or on your right, you have two tricks; the more points partner has, the more likely it is that the ace is there; holdings like J-x-x or 10-9-x also boost the probability of your taking two tricks.

The **LTC** does not measure certain winners but only the potential of the hands. Counting A-Q-x or K-Q-x as one loser / two winners, which it will be four times out of five, is clearly a sensible estimate.

With weaker holdings such as K-x-x or Q-J-x or Q-10-x, the same reasoning can be used to demonstrate that the probable outcome will be two losers / one winner rather than three losers / no winners. As long as it is appreciated that we are talking in terms of probabilities and not certainties, no damage is done by referring to A-Q-x / K-Q-x as two tricks and K-x-x / Q-J-x / Q-10-x as one trick, and so on.

Example Hands

	WEST	EAST	
1 loser	♠ K Q 8 6 4 3	♠ A 5 2	2 losers
1 loser	♡ A K 6	♡ Q 9 2	2½ losers
1 loser	◇ 7	◇ Q J 3	2 losers
1 loser	♣ A Q 2	♣ K 9 4 3	2 losers
4 losers			8½ losers

WEST	EAST
1♠	2NT (1)
3♠ (2)	4♠ (3)
4NT	5◇
6♠	Pass

(1) 11-12 points, therefore around 8 losers.

(2) With 4 losers opposite an expected 8-loser hand, West should explore the slam rather than sign off in 4 Spades. As the cards lie, the slam is laydown. On a different layout, the slam might require a finesse. Even if you interchange the minor suits, the slam is still around 70%.

(3) 4♣, 4◇ or 4♡ here would be a cue bid with support for spades.

	WEST	EAST	
2 losers	♠ K 9 4 3	♠ A Q 6	1 loser
2 losers	♡ K 7 5	♡ A Q J 8 4 3	1 loser
1 loser	◇ A 7	◇ 8	1 loser
1 loser	♣ A Q 10 2	♣ 9 8 3	3 losers
6 losers			6 losers

WEST	EAST
1NT (1)	3♡ (2)
4♣ (3)	4NT (4)
5♣ (5)	6♡
Pass	

(1) 15-17 points, therefore around 6 losers.
(2) With a good suit and 6 losers opposite an expected 6 losers, East looks for a slam.
(3) Cue bid showing the ace of clubs and support for hearts.
(4) Roman Key Card Blackwood.
(5) 0 or 3 key cards. East can deduce this to show the two missing aces and the king of trumps.

Summary

To calculate the playing strength of the partnership hands after a trump fit has been found :

> *Count Your Losers*
> *Add Partner's Losers*
> *Deduct the Total from 24*
> *Answer = Tricks Expected*

Count no more than three losers per suit. Count the A, K and Q as winners, cards below the queen as losers. Count the supported queen as a winner but count a three-card or longer suit with the queen and no other honour as $2\frac{1}{2}$ losers.

Partner's losers are estimated by counting a minimum opening as seven losers. If partner opens and you have seven losers, game is likely to succeed if a trump fit is found. If partner opens and you have five losers, slam potential exists if a trump fit is found.

When you start applying the **LTC**, be satisfied for the time being with a RAW COUNT. Once you have had some experience with this

RAW COUNT, you will want to progress to the more advanced valuation techniques and refinements discussed in Chapter 10, Adjustments To The Losing Trick Count.

Quiz

1. *How many losers for each of these card combinations?*

a. J 7 3   **b.** Q 10 4   **c.** 8 3   **d.** A K 4 3 2

e. A Q 9 8   **f.** 8 6 3 2   **g.** K Q J 6 4 2   **h.** A J

2. *How many losers do these hands have?*

a. ♠ K Q 8 7 3	**b.** ♠ A 8 7	**c.** ♠ K Q 9	**d.** ♠ Q J 9
♡ A 3	♡ A 9	♡ A Q 7 6 3 2	♡ A Q 6 2
◇ A J 5 4 2	◇ K 7 6 3	◇ A 3 2	◇ 8 4
♣ 7	♣ Q J 5 4	♣ 7	♣ 9 6 3 2

Answers

1. **a.** 3   **b.** 2   **c.** 2   **d.** 1   **e.** 1   **f.** 3   **g.** 1   **h.** 1

2. **a.** 5   **b.** 7   **c.** 5   **d.** 8

3
Summary of Losers in Standard Methods

1. Raising Opener's Major

1♡ : 2♡ or 1♠ : 2♠ – 6-10 points, 8 or 9 losers.

1♡ : 3♡ or 1♠ : 3♠ –
The partnership will need to stipulate whether this is played as a limit raise (10-12 points, 8 losers) or as a game-force (7 losers or better).

1♡ : 4♡ or 1♠ : 4♠ – 7 losers and normally 6-10 HCP.

Pass : 1♡, 3♡ or Pass : 1♠, 3♠ –
10-12 points and 8 losers. Equivalent to the limit raise.

2. Raising Opener's Minor

1♣ : 2♣ or 1◇ : 2◇ – 6-10 points, 8-9 losers, no major suit.
1♣ : 2♣ or 1◇ : 2◇ –
Limit raise = 10-12 points, 8 losers, no major suit.
Game-forcing raise = 13 points or more, 7 losers or better, no major.

3. Raising Opener's Rebid

At the one-level, e.g. 1♣ : 1♡, 1♠ : ? –
Raising to the two-level is the same as raising opener's major to the two-level initially, 6-10 points and 8-9 losers.

Raising to the three-level is normally played as a limit raise, based on 10-12 points and 8 losers, though the partnership can stipulate it to be game-forcing, 13 or more points, 7 losers or better.

Raising to game shows a 7-loser hand without ambitions for slam.

Where opener rebids at the two-level after a one-over-one response :
After, for example, 1♡ : 1♠, 2♣ : ?
Pass or 2♡, simple preference = 9 losers or worse.
3♣ or 3♡, genuine raise = 8 losers, not forcing.
4♡ = 7 losers, game values. 4♣ = 6 losers or better. The jump to 4-minor is normally played as game-forcing with slam ambitions.

Opener rebids after a two-over-one response :
   1♠ : 2♣, 2◇ : ?
   3◇ is non-forcing in old-style standard and would show 8 losers. In many modern systems, the two-over-response is played as a game-force so that the expectancy is 7 losers or better. The jump raise to 4◇ is played as game-forcing with slam ambitions, 6 losers or better.
   Reverting to the major, 2♠, is non-forcing in old-style standard and would therefore show an 8-loser hand. Jumping to 3♠ over 2◇ would be a game-force with 7 losers or better.

4. Raising Responder

Response at the one-level, 6 or more points, = 9-10 losers or better.
Raising responder's one-level response :
   To the two-level, e.g. 1◇ : 1♠, 2♠ = 12-15 points and 7 losers.
   To the three-level, e.g. 1♣ : 1♡, 3♡ = 16-18 points and 6 losers.
   To the four-level, e.g. 1◇ : 1♠, 4♠ = 19 or more points, 5 losers.
   With an even stronger raise, opener should jump-shift first and support responder's major on the next round, thus indicating the values for at least game and about a 4-loser hand.

Response at the two-level, 10 points or more, = 8 losers or better.

Raising a minor suit response :
   To the three-level, e.g. 1♡ : 2♣, 3♣ = 12-15 points, 6-7 losers.
   To the four-level, e.g. 1♠ : 2◇, 4◇ = 5 losers or better, forcing to game and suggesting slam possibilities.

Raising a response of 2♡ after a 1♠ opening :
   To the three-level, 1♠ : 2♡, 3♡ = is non-forcing in old-style standard and would show a 7-loser hand.
   To the four-level, 1♠ : 2♡, 4♡ = would show a 6-loser or better hand in old-style standard.
   This approach is awkward since opener has trouble showing very good support for hearts and significantly extra values, such as a 5-loser or better hand with slam prospects. The modern style is to play 1♠ : 2♡, 4♡ as a 7-loser hand and 1♠ : 2♡, 3♡ as 6 losers or better, forcing to game.
   This in turn led to the bolstering of the two-over-one response and where the two-over-one is played as game-forcing, the expectancy would be 7 losers or better. This minimum requirement would naturally carry over to responder's subsequent rebids.

[27]

5. Opener's Strong Actions

Opener's reverse, e.g. 1♣ : 1♠, 2♡, should indicate 16 points or more, an unbalanced shape with the first bid suit definitely longer than the second, and a hand of 5 losers or better. If the high card content falls below 15, a reverse is still acceptable if the hand has no more than 5 losers. 6-5 patterns may reverse even on 12-13 points with a loser count of 4.

Opener's jump rebid in the suit opened, e.g. 1♣ : 1♡, 3♣, should have about 16-18 points and 5-6 losers. This action is not forcing after a one-over-one response and therefore a hand with 4 losers would be too strong.

Opener's jump shift, e.g. 1♣ : 1♡, 2♠ or 1♡ : 1♠, 3♢, is a force to game and should show a 4-loser hand. The point count is usually 19 or more but a hand with fewer points is acceptable if the 4-loser requirement is met.

Opener's very strong openings would show a 3-loser or better hand if the opening is forcing to game. If the opening is forcing for one round but not forcing to game, the expectancy would be between $3\frac{1}{2}$ and $4\frac{1}{2}$ losers, so that a contract at the three-level is reasonable.

6. Weak Twos and Higher Pre-empts

Minimum weak two = 6-8 HCP and 8 losers
Maximum weak two = 8-10 HCP and 7 losers

Pre-emptive openings at the 3-level, 4-level or 5-minor-level are normally based on 6-10 HCP and a 7-card or longer suit. The high card content may be less if the loser requirement is fulfilled. Likewise, the suit length may be reduced if the loser requirement is satisfied.

3-opening not vulnerable	:	7 losers
3-opening vulnerable	:	6 losers
4-opening not vulnerable	:	6 losers
4-opening vulnerable	:	5 losers
5-Minor not vulnerable	:	5 losers
5-Minor vulnerable	:	4 losers

7. No-Trump Openings, Responses and Rebids

The **LTC** does not claim to operate for no-trump hands, but it is still vital to know the expectancy of partner's no-trump hand type in terms of losers so that if a trump fit does come to light, the loser expectancy can be gauged.

12-14 1NT = 7-8 losers, commonly 8
13-15 1NT = 7-8 losers, commonly 7
14-17 1NT = 6-7 losers, 7 if minimum, 6 if maximum
15-18 1NT = 6-7 losers, commonly 6
16-18 1NT = normally 6 losers
19-20-21 range = normally 5 losers
22-23-24 range = normally 4 losers

The above is a guideline only for balanced hands and naturally the same loser count would apply for no-trump responses in the above ranges. The 1NT response of 6-9 points is 9-10 losers (usually 9) and a 2NT response/rebid in the 11-12 range is around 8 losers.

8. Overcalls and Takeout Doubles

Standard Overcalls :

At the 1-level, 8-15 HCP and a good suit = 8 losers up to 6 losers.

At the 2-level, but not a jump overcall, 10-15 HCP and a good suit = 7 losers up to 6 losers, very rarely 8 losers or 5 losers.

Weak jump overcall, 6-10 HCP + 6-card or longer suit = 7-8 losers.

Intermediate jump overcall, 11-15 HCP + 6-card or longer suit, in other words it is equivalent to a minimum opening hand with a good, rebiddable suit = 6-7 losers.

Strong jump overcall, 15-18 HCP + a good suit = 5-6 losers.

The partnership will stipulate whether weak, intermediate or strong jump overcalls are to be used. If the partnership is using standard overcalls with either weak or intermediate jump overcalls, hands which are too strong for these actions are shown via a takeout double.

Takeout double = 7 losers or better.

Takeout doubler who bids again opposite weak response = 5 losers.

Takeout double + jump opposite weak response = 4 losers.

The above 5-loser and 4-loser requirements apply whether the doubler is supporting partner or bidding a new suit.

Responding to the takeout double :

9 losers or worse = Bid a suit at cheapest level or 1NT.

8 losers = Jump in a suit or jump to 2NT.

7 losers = Bid game in your suit or explore game via a cue bid of the opponents' suit.

All of the above will be examined in detail in subsequent chapters.

4

Raising Opener's Suit

Major-Suit Raises

1. Responder has 8 or 9 losers :

The Single Raise – 1♡ : 2♡ or 1♠ : 2♠

    This is played much the same way in all systems, about 6-10 points and support for opener. From the **LTC** point of view, *responder's single raise will contain 8 or 9 losers*. For example,

♠ K 7 6 4	♠ A 7 6 2
♡ K Q 8 3	♡ Q J 4 2
◇ 7 4 3	◇ 7 3
♣ 6 5	♣ 8 6 5
8 losers	9 losers

    Clearly a hand which had 7 losers would be too strong for a single raise, since opener would be expected to hold 7 losers and game could normally be made (7 + 7 = 14, 24 — 14 = 10 tricks).

2. Responder holds 7 losers :

    Where responder has support and 7 losers, responder's action will vary according to the high card strength held and the system being used.

    1♡:4♡ or 1♠:4♠ is pretty standard and a normal game raise can be expected to have 6-10 HCP and 7 losers. For example, if partner opens 1♠, bid 4♠ on each of these hands :

♠ K 7 6 4 3	♠ K Q 4 3	♠ K 8 7 2
♡ 8	♡ A 7 5 4 2	♡ 3
◇ 7 2	◇ 3	◇ 9 8 6 5 4 2
♣ A 7 4 3 2	♣ 7 6 2	♣ A 3

    Fewer HCP are permissible as long as 7 losers are held. Some texts call these "gambling raises" but the gamble is a pretty good one since with a good trump fit and seven losers opposite an opening hand, ten tricks will be made most of the time, according to the **LTC**. Suppose the hands were :

♠ A Q 8 5 2   ♠ K 7 6 4 3
♥ A Q 2   ♥ 8
♦ 8 6 5   ♦ 7 2
♣ 9 8   ♣ A 7 4 3 2

Despite having only 19 HCP, the hands will make 4 ♠ easily. Note that the 1 ♠ opening is quite minimum, only 12 HCP, no short suit and no exceptional length, but it does have seven losers.

Holding support for opener's major, seven losers and more than 10 HCP, responders will use the 1 ♥ : 3 ♥ or 1 ♠ : 3 ♠ raise if this is played as forcing *or* may use a *splinter bid* (see later) if that is available in the partnership's system *or* may change suit first, jump to game later (the delayed-game-raise) if 1 ♥ : 3 ♥ or 1 ♠ : 3 ♠ is used as a limit raise (see later).

3. Responder has 6 losers or better :

With support and 6 losers or better, responder is too strong to jump to game at once via 1♥ : 4♥ or 1♠ : 4♠. Responder would choose a jump-raise (1♥ : 3♥ or 1♠ : 3♠) if played as forcing *or* perhaps a splinter *or* whatever other strong action is available within the system.

4. Responder has 10 losers or worse :

From time to time, you will have support for opener, 6-10 points but 10 losers. For example, after a 1 ♠ opening :

♠ K 7 5 3 ♠ J 7 6 5 ♠ Q J 8 6
♥ 9 4 2   ♥ A 3   ♥ Q 4 3
♦ J 4 3   ♦ J 4 2   ♦ 7 6 2
♣ A 7 6   ♣ J 6 3 2 ♣ Q 4 2

10 losers   10 losers   10 losers

These are quite common problems. In standard systems, you should simply tolerate this situation. Give the 1 ♠ : 2 ♠ single raise on the above hands, but allow opener to base further action on an expectancy of the normal 8-9 loser hand. (If your shape is 4-3-3-3 and your strength lies outside partner's suit, a standard response of 1NT is advisable.) When opener invites game after 1-Major : 2 Major and you have a 10-loser hand, you should almost invariably reject the invitation.

Systems which employ a *forcing* 1NT response (e.g. Precision, Roth-Stone, Kaplan-Sheinwold and derivatives of these) can surmount this problem. The direct 1-Major : 2-Major raise shows 8-9 losers. The 1NT response, forcing, followed by two-level support (e.g. 1♡ : 1NT, 2♣ : 2♡) shows the 10-loser type, a hand too weak to give a direct raise to 2-Major. (The same sequence is also used in those systems to show a possibly stronger hand but with only doubleton support for opener.)

Where responder has support for opener but 11 or 12 losers, responder should pass unless planning a psychic bid. Game will not be a proposition, since opposite an 11-loser hand, opener would need to hold a 3-loser hand and with such strength, opener would be too strong for just a 1-opening.

Subsequent Bidding After a Raise

After 1♡ : 2♡ or 1♠ : 2♠ (responder has 8 or 9 losers) :

Opener's strategy :

With 7 losers	: *Pass*
With 6 losers	: *Invite game*
With 5 losers	: *Head for game*

For example :

♠ A Q 8 6 4	♠ A K 7 4 3	♠ A 9 6 5 4
♡ J 6	♡ 8 3	♡ 7
♢ K Q 6	♢ J 8 6 2	♢ A K Q 3 2
♣ J 4 3	♣ A K	♣ 4 3
7 losers	6 losers	5 losers
1♠ : 2♠	1♠ : 2♠	1♠ : 2♠
Pass	3♢ – Trial bid	4♠

With 7 losers facing 8 or 9 losers, the total will be 15 or 16 losers, and thus 8 or 9 tricks. The **LTC** indicates that 10 tricks are improbable so that there is no benefit in bidding beyond the two-level.

Where opener holds 5 losers opposite 8 there should be potential for 11 tricks while opposite 9 losers, the likely outcome is 10 tricks. In either case, game is a good chance and so you should simply bid the game. There is no value in giving extra information to the opposition.

The really interesting case is when opener holds 6 losers with which you should invite game. 6 losers opposite 9 = 15 losers or 9 tricks, but 6 opposite 8 means 14 losers or 10 tricks. Since game is possible but not certain, you should make some effort to reach game in case responder has the better kind of raise.

The available choices are :

Raise the major again (1♡ : 2♡, 3♡   or   1♠ : 2♠, 3♠)

Bid 2NT

Bid a new suit as a trial bid

Which of these actions you should choose will vary according to the degree of sophistication of the partnership. In standard methods, the meanings given to these actions are :

The Re-Raise (1♡ : 2♡, 3♡   or   1♠ : 2♠, 3♠)
"Bid four if you are maximum, pass if you are minimum."

The 2NT Rebid (1♡ : 2♡, 2NT   or   1♠ : 2♠, 2NT)
"I have a no-trump type of hand. If you are minimum, pass if you fancy no-trumps or bid 3-of-our-major if you do not like no-trumps. If you are maximum, bid game, either 3NT if your hand is suitable for no-trumps or 4-of-our-major if you prefer a suit contract."

New Suit = Trial Bid (e.g. 1♡ : 2♡, 3♣   or   1♠ : 2♠, 3♢)
The most popular version of this method is the Long Suit Trial Bid : "I have three or more cards in this suit and this is where help is needed most. With a good holding in the trial suit, bid game-in-our-major, but with a weak holding, bid only 3-of-our-major as a sign-off."

Where the opener holds a 5-loser hand which contains a suit which has three losers, it will normally pay the opener to utilise the long suit trial. With only 5 losers one would expect game to be a good bet, but a 3-loser suit facing the same with partner often puts paid to game chances.

Some partnerships use Short Suit Trial Bids. In this method after 1♡ : 2♡ or 1♠ : 2♠, a new suit says, "This is my singleton. If your values include no wasted strength (or little wasted strength) opposite my short suit, bid game-in-our-major, but if you do have wasted values opposite the shortage, sign-off in 3-of-our-major."

Using the **LTC**, you are able to give much more accurate definition to the Trial Bids and the responses to them.

Long Suit Trials

After 1♡ : 2♡ or 1♠ : 2♠, a new suit says, "I have three or more cards in this suit *with two or three losers.*" Do not make a trial bid in a strong suit (two or three top honours) or in a short suit. With such a holding, choose a different invitational bid.

K-x-x-x, A-x-x, x-x-x-x, J-x-x, Q-x-x are suitable suits for trial bids.

A-Q-x-x, K-J-10-x, A-J-10-x, x-x are unsuitable – they are too strong.

Responder's reply to the long suit trial :

0 losers in the trial suit	:	Bid game in your major
1 loser in the trial suit	:	Bid game in your major
2 losers in the trial suit	:	Bid game if maximum, sign-off in 3-of-your-major if minimum
3 losers in the trial suit	:	Sign-off in 3-of-your-major

With three losers in the trial suit but a maximum raise, you may bid a new suit below 3-of-your-major provided that you have considerable strength in this new suit. For example, 1♠ : 2♠, 3♣ : 3♡ would say "I cannot help you in clubs but I am keen on game and my main outside strength is located in hearts." This is known as a counter-trial which always shows maximum values for the raise to the two-level. Over the counter-trial, opener can bid game if the values revealed are suitable. Otherwise opener will sign-off in 3-of-the-major.

After 1♡ : 2♡, what action should opener take with these hands?

		a.		b.		c.
		♠ A 7		♠ 7		♠ 7 2
		♡ A Q 6 4 2		♡ A K 8 5 3		♡ K 8 7 4 2
		◇ 8 7 6 2		◇ A 7 6		◇ A Q J
		♣ K Q		♣ K 8 3 2		♣ K Q 3

Answers :

(a) 3 Diamonds, trial bid in your weak suit.

(b) 3 Clubs. With two trial suits available, choose the weaker suit, the suit in which you need help most.

(c) 3 Hearts. You have no suit justifying a long suit trial. Do not make a long suit trial in a strong suit or a short suit.

Example Hands on Long Suit Trials

WEST	EAST		WEST	EAST
♠ 9 6	♠ 8 7 3 2		♠ 9 6	♠ 8 7 3 2
♡ A Q J 5 4	♡ K 7 3 2		♡ A Q J 5 4	♡ K 7 3 2
◇ A 2	◇ 7 5 4		◇ A 2	◇ K 5
♣ A 6 3 2	♣ K 5		♣ A 6 3 2	♣ 7 5 4

WEST	EAST		WEST	EAST
1♡	2♡		1♡	2♡
3♣ (1)	4♡ (2)		3♣ (1)	3♡ (2)
Pass			Pass	

(1) Long Suit trial bid
(2) Only one loser in the trial suit – bid game in your major.

(1) Long suit trial bid
(2) Three losers in the trial suit – sign-off in 3-of-your-major.

WEST	EAST		WEST	EAST
♠ 9 6	♠ Q J 8 2		♠ 9 6	♠ Q J 8 2
♡ A Q J 5 4	♡ K 7 3 2		♡ A Q J 5 4	♡ K 7 3 2
◇ A 2	◇ 7 5 4		◇ A 2	◇ K 5 4
♣ A 6 3 2	♣ 7 5		♣ A 6 3 2	♣ 7 5

WEST	EAST		WEST	EAST
1♡	2♡		1♡	2♡
3♣ (1)	3♡ (2)		3♣ (1)	4♡ (2)
Pass			Pass	

(1) Long suit trial bid
(2) Two losers in the trial suit – sign-off in 3-major if minimum.

(1) Long suit trial bid
(2) Two losers in the trial suit – bid game in the major if maximum.

WEST	EAST		WEST	EAST
♠ A K Q 8 6 2	♠ J 5 4 3		♠ A K Q 8 6 2	♠ J 7 5 3
♡ 4 2	♡ A K 6		♡ K Q 2	♡ A 6
◇ J 6 3	◇ 9 8 2		◇ 7	◇ Q 6 4
♣ A 2	♣ Q 6 4		♣ J 6 3	♣ 8 5 4 2

WEST	EAST		WEST	EAST
1♠	2♠		1♠	2♠
3◇ (1)	3♡ (2)		3♣ (1)	3♠ (2)
3NT (3)	Pass		Pass	

(1) Long suit trial bid
(2) Counter-trial : Cannot help you in diamonds but my hand is maximum with strength in hearts.
(3) This looks a good bet.

(1) Even with 5 losers, a trial bid is appropriate with a 3-loser suit.
(2) With three losers in the trial suit, sign-off if minimum. Do not make a counter-trial.

Short Suit Trials

In this method, after 1♡ : 2♡ or 1♠ : 2♠, a new suit says, "This is my singleton. Bid game if the fit is good, sign-off if the fit is bad."

A good fit is to hold *no wasted high cards* opposite the short suit. Ideal are holdings like x-x-x, x-x-x-x, J-x-x, J-x-x-x, A-x-x or longer. Moderate holdings are A-x and x-x and poor holdings are K-Q, K-Q-x or longer, K-x-x or longer, Q-J-x or longer and Q-x-x or longer.

Responder's reply to the short suit trial :

3 losers in the trial suit	: Bid game in your major
Ace + 2 losers in the trial suit	: Bid game in your major
No ace + 2 losers in the trial suit	: Bid game if maximum, sign-off in 3-major if minimum
Ace + 1 loser in the trial suit	: Bid game if maximum, sign-off in 3-major if minimum
No ace + 1 loser in the trial suit	: Sign-off in 3-major

Example Hands on Short Suit Trials

WEST	EAST	WEST	EAST
♠ K 9 8 6 4	♠ A 5 3 2	♠ K 9 8 6 4	♠ A 5 3 2
♡ A J 10	♡ K 6 5	♡ A J 10	♡ 4 2
◇ K Q 6 2	◇ 4 3	◇ K Q 6 2	◇ 8 5 4 3
♣ 7	♣ 8 5 4 3	♣ 7	♣ K 6 5

WEST	EAST	WEST	EAST
1♠	2♠	1♠	2♠
3♣ (1)	4♠ (2)	3♣ (1)	3♠ (2)
Pass		Pass	

(1) Short suit trial bid
(2) No wastage in the trial suit – bid game in your major.

(1) Short suit trial bid
(2) Two losers in the trial suit and no ace – sign-off if minimum.

WEST	EAST	WEST	EAST
♠ 7	♠ 9 6 5 2	♠ 7	♠ K Q 9 2
♡ A J 7 4 3	♡ K Q 9 2	♡ A J 7 4 3	♡ 9 6 5 2
◇ A K 2	◇ Q 6 5	◇ A K 2	◇ Q 6 5
♣ Q J 10 2	♣ 8 3	♣ Q J 10 2	♣ 8 3

WEST	EAST	WEST	EAST
1♡	2♡	1♡	2♡
2♠ (1)	4♡ (2)	2♠ (1)	3♡ (2)
Pass		Pass	

(1) Short suit trial bid
(2) Three losers in the trial suit – bid game in your major.

(1) Short suit trial bid
(2) One loser in the trial suit and no ace – sign-off in 3-major.

How to Use Both Long Suit Trials and Short Suit Trials

Long Suit Trials and Short Suit Trials are both valuable when the appropriate hands arise and are more accurate in game bidding than the momma-poppa 1-Major : 2-Major, 3-Major. If you examine the example hands on page 35 and 36, you will note the loss in accuracy if each of the auctions began 1-Major : 2-Major, 3-Major.

Whether you use Long Suit Trials or Short Suit Trials will be decided in advance by the partnership. Long Suit Trials are the more popular. However, using only Long Suit Trials, you can be stuck when you have no suitable weak suit for a trial bid. Likewise, if you use only Short Suit Trials, you may not hold a singleton. Would if not be attractive if one could use both Long Suit Trials *and* Short Suit Trials?

The method whereby one can use Long Suit Trials or Short Suit Trials according to the dictates of the hand requires one to give up the natural meaning of 2NT in the 1-Major : 2-Major, 2NT auctions but this is no great loss. After a major suit fit has been found, few hands warrant a no-trumps contract as opposed to the known major fit and a significant drawback to using 2NT for a balanced hand invitation is the information given to the opposition, as this may assist them greatly in the defence if partner returns to the major suit.

The Long Suit Trials / Short Suit Trials Method :

After 1♠ : 2♠ –

2NT = Short suit relay : "I am about to make a short suit trial bid. Please bid 3♣." After partner bids the forced 3♣ ("puppet") opener bids :

3◇ = Singleton diamond

3♡ = Singleton heart

3♠ = Singleton club. Since spades is the trump suit, you do not wish to bid beyond 3♠ until you have the relevant information. Therefore 3♠ becomes a short suit trial in the unavailable suit, clubs.

If responder refuses to take the 3♣ puppet, responder is showing a singleton (e.g. 3◇ = singleton diamond, 3♡ = singleton heart, 3♠ = singleton club) and leaving it to opener to make the decision.

Any new suit by opener after 1♠ : 2♠ is a long suit trial.

After 1♡ : 2♡ –

2♠ = Short suit relay : "I am about to make a short suit trial. Please bid 2NT." After responder bids the forced 2NT ("puppet"), opener bids :

3♣ = Singleton club

3◇ = Singleton diamond

3♡ = Singleton spade. Since hearts is the trump suit, you do not wish to bid beyond 3♡ until you have the relevant information. Therefore, 3♡ becomes a short suit trial in the unavailable suit, spades.

If responder refuses to take the puppet, responder is showing a singleton (e.g. 3♣ = singleton club, 3◇ = singleton diamond, 3♡ = singleton spade) and leaving it to opener to make the decision.

3♣ or 3◇ by opener over 2♡ = Long suit trial in the suit bid.
2NT by opener over 2♡ = Long suit trial in spades (because 2♠ is the short suit relay).

Where opener indicates the desire to make a short suit trial and responder refuses the puppet, responder should not hold a hand with which a clearcut decision would be made when opener's singleton is revealed. With such a hand, responder should obviously make the puppet bid and discover opener's singleton suit.

Where opener bids the short suit relay, it is conceivable that responder has a hand which would accept the invitation no matter which singleton opener held. In such a case, responder does not take the puppet but simply bids game in the major (e.g. 1♡ : 2♡, 2♠ : 4♡). There is no point in letting the opponents know opener's singleton.

Summary : After 1-Major : 2-Major, the next bid operates as a relay, requiring responder to bid the next step over which opener makes a short suit trial. Refusal by responder to take the puppet shows that responder has a singleton. When responder does take the puppet, opener bids the short suit. If opener bids 3-of-the-agreed major, this is a short suit trial in the unavailable suit. Actions by opener below 3-major other than the short suit relay are long suit trials.

Combining Long Suit Trials and Short Suit Trials is not for casual partnerships. For a seasoned, regular partnership with no memory problems, the above is a definite advance on standard methods.

Bidding After a Jump Raise

(A) Limit Raises

These are commonly used in the Acol System and in many Standard American partnerships. In this method :

1-Major : 3-Major = 10-12 points and precisely 8 losers

The limit raise is not forcing but is strongly invitational. It must not be 7 losers (too strong, game is likely) or 9 losers (too weak). It should not have 13 or more points (too strong) or less than 10 points (too weak – prefer to use 1-Major : 2-Major). The jump raise by a passed hand (Pass : 1-Major, 3-Major) is typically a limit raise of 10-12 points and 8 losers, no more, no less. The limit raise should include four trumps.

Opener's action after the limit raise (facing 8 losers) :

With a bare 7 losers : Pass
(7 + 8 = 15; 24 – 15 = 9 tricks only)

With $6\frac{1}{2}$ – 5 losers : Bid game in the major
($6\frac{1}{2} + 8 = 14\frac{1}{2}$; $24 – 14\frac{1}{2} = 9\frac{1}{2}$ tricks, so that game should be at least a 50-50 chance. 5 + 8 = 13; 24 – 13 = 11 tricks expected, so that a slam is unlikely to succeed.)

With 4½ losers or better : Bid slam or explore slam
(With 4 losers for example, 4 + 8 = 12; 24 – 12 = 12 tricks potential.) If
you have the necessary controls, you can simply bid 6-of-your-major.
The necessary controls would be first round control in all suits or three
first round controls and second round control in the fourth suit.

♠ K 8 6 4	WEST	EAST	♠ A Q 9 7 5 3
♡ K 4	Pass	1 ♠	♡ A 6
◇ A J 8 3	3 ♠	6 ♠	◇ 2
♣ 7 5 4	Pass		♣ A K 6 2

On other hands with slam potential, the slam exploration will
depend on the partnership's methods. At least three sensible methods
exist :

(a) Slam Trials

These are like long suit game trials except that the suit need not be as
weak. A new suit after 1 ♡ : 3 ♡ or 1 ♠ : 3 ♠ says, "I am interested in
slam if you have a fit with this suit. If you cannot fit this suit, sign-off in
4-of-our major, but if you have a strong holding in this suit, bid
anything else (e.g. a suit where you have the ace or raise the trial suit)."

OPENER	Responder A	Responder B
♠ A K J 6 4	♠ Q 10 7 2	♠ Q 10 7 2
♡ A 2	♡ K Q	♡ Q 5
◇ A 9 8 4 3	◇ 6 5 2	◇ K J 2
♣ 7	♣ A 6 4 3	♣ A 6 4 3

After 1 ♠ : 3 ♠, opener makes a slam trial with 4 ◇. Responder A,
with nothing in the trial suit, should sign off in 4 ♠. Responder B, with
a strong holding in the trial suit, should cue bid 5 ♣ and the
partnership should reach the excellent slam in spades.

(b) 3NT as Blackwood

After 1-Major : 3-Major, it makes little sense to reserve 3NT as a
natural bid since it is so rare that one would want to play in 3NT after a
major suit has been strongly supported. Even if 3NT happened to be
the correct spot, it would be almost impossible for either partner to
judge that with any degree of confidence.

Accordingly, opener's 3NT rebid can be used as the partnership's
preferred version of Blackwood. Recommended would be Roman Key
Card Blackwood where the replies to the 3NT ask would be :

4♣ = 0 or 3 key cards
4◇ = 1 key card
4♡ = 2 key cards, no queen of trumps
4♠ = 2 key cards and the queen of trumps

The five key cards are the four aces and the king of trumps. A limit raise could not, of course, hold four or five key cards, 3NT Roman Key Card Blackwood works well in conjunction with Slam Trials.

OPENER	Responder A	Responder B
♠ K J 8 6 5	♠ A 7 4 2	♠ A Q 7 4
♡ A Q	♡ K 8 3	♡ 8 3 2
◇ K Q J 4 2	◇ 8 3	◇ A 8
♣ 7	♣ K J 9 6	♣ J 9 6 2

After 1♠ : 3♠, opener uses 3NT RKCB (the diamond suit is too solid for a slam trial). Responder A replies 4◇, showing one key card. Opener knows that two aces are missing and signs off in 4♠. A contract of 5♠ might make but is in jeopardy. Responder B would reply 4♠ showing two key cards and the queen of trumps. That is enough for the opener to bid the excellent slam in spades.

(c) New suit as a cue bid with 3NT as a relay

In this method, a new suit promises the ace or void in the suit bid and asks partner to bid the cheapest suit outside trumps in which the ace (or a void) is held. Standard cue bidding can be used in conjunction with 3NT as RKCB as above. An attractive alternative is to utilise 3NT as a relay, denying the ace of clubs. Thus –

1♠ : 3♠, 3NT denies the ace of clubs.
1♠ : 3♠, 4◇ shows the ace of diamonds *and* the ace of clubs.
(This logically follows since 3NT denying the ♣A was not used.)
1♠ : 3♠, 4♣ shows the ace of clubs and denies the ace of diamonds (since 4◇ was not bid).
Hence, 1♠ : 3♠, 4♡ would show the ♡A, ◇A *and* ♣A.
Likewise –
1♡ : 3♡, 3♠ shows the ace of spades (with no other promises).
1♡ : 3♡, 3NT denies the ace of spades *and* denies the ace of clubs.
1♡ : 3♡, 4♣ promises the ace of clubs and denies the ace of spades, as well as denying the ace of diamonds.
1♡ : 3♡, 4◇ promises the ace of diamonds and the ace of clubs, and denies the ace of spades.

Relay cue bidding is recommended only for a regular partnership.

(B) Pre-emptive Jump Raises

In this style, the 1-Major : 3-Major raises are played as pre-emptive rather than constructive. They show about 6-9 HCP, four-card support for opener and 8 losers. Naturally, partnerships using this approach have other ways to describe their constructive raises.

After a pre-emptive jump raise, slam would be a rarity but feasible if opener had a freak two-suiter. Opener could take the same approach as after a limit raise with considerable conservatism in exploring a slam.

OPENER	Responder A	Responder B
♠ A 9 8 6 4 3	♠ K J 7 5	♠ K 7 5 2
♡ 7	♡ Q J 8 5 4	♡ A 3
◇ K Q J 5 2	◇ 8 3	◇ 8 4
♣ A	♣ 9 6	♣ 9 8 6 4 2

After 1♠ : 3♠, opener could trot out 3NT as Roman Key Card Blackwood. Responder A would show just one key card and opener would sign off in 4♠. Responder B would reveal two key cards, enabling opener to bid the excellent 6♠.

(C) Game-Forcing Jump Raises

Where 1-Major : 3-Major is played as forcing to game, it usually promises 13 or more points and should indicate a hand with 7 losers or better. If this approach is used, then the 10-12 point 8-loser raise requires a different treatment. The common choices are :

a. Make a natural two-level response first and support the major later (e.g. 1♡ : 2♣, 2♡ : 3♡ or 1♡ : 2♣, 2◇ : 2♡).

b. Use the 1NT forcing response and jumps to 3-of-the-major with your rebid (e.g. 1♠ : 1NT, 2◇ : 3♠).

c. Make an *artificial* 2♣ response showing 10-12 points and support partner's major on the next round.

Opener's action after 1-Major : 3-Major forcing to game :

With 7 losers : Bid 4-of-the-major.

With 6 losers : Slam is possible if partner has better than 7 losers.
Since the forcing jump raise shows 7 losers *or better*, opener should sign off in game with a minimum opening. With a better hand, opener should indicate slam interest without committing the partnership to

slam. This can be achieved by making a cue bid (this shows the slam interest) but not venturing beyond the four-level. If possible, make only one cue bid and then sign off in 4-of-the-major. For example :

1♡	:	3♡	*or*	1♠	:	3♠
4♣	:	4◇		4♣	:	4♡
4♡ ...				4♠ ...		

With 5 losers or better : Slam is now highly likely.
(5 + 7 = 12; 24 – 12 = 12 tricks potential). Either use Blackwood 4NT (or Gerber 4♣ if you are unable to resist this convention) or start a cue bidding sequence. After cue bidding has started, do not sign off in 4-of-the-major (this would show the 6-loser hand) unless it is already obvious that two aces are missing. Taking a cue bidding auction to the five-level indicates that the values for slam are there but either that control in one of the suits may be critical or that perhaps a grand slam is in the offing. For example, if the bidding so far has been 1♠ : 3♠, 4♡ : 5♣, 5♠ . . ". opener is indicating that slam values are present but that the diamond suit is the problem. With neither first round nor second round control in diamonds, responder will pass 5♠, but with such control, responder will bid on.

Responder's Further Actions

After 1♡ : 3♡, 4♡ *or* 1♠ : 3♠, 4♠ –

Opener has shown 7 losers. If responder has 6 or 7 losers, responder should pass (7 + 7 = 14; 24 – 14 = 10 tricks only; 6 + 7 = 13; 24 – 13 = 11 tricks potential, slam unlikely).

With 5 losers, responder should push on towards slam despite opener's signoff (5 + 7 = 12; 24 – 12 = 12 tricks potential). Use Blackwood 4NT (Roman Key Card Blackwood is preferred) or start a cue bidding sequence if this is indicated by the problems of the hand.

After 1-Major : 3-Major, followed by a cue bid by opener :

With 7 losers, cue bid below 4-of-your-major or, if that is not possible, sign off in 4-of-your-major. Do not push beyond 4-of-your-major yourself with no better than a 7-loser hand. For example :

1♡	:	3♡	*or*	1♡	:	3♡	*or*	1♡	:	3♡	*or*	1♡	:	3♡
4♣	:	4◇		4♣	:	4♡		3♠	:	4♣		4♣	:	4◇
								4◇	:	4♡		4♡	:	Pass

With 6 losers, cue bid at the cheapest level and be prepared to go beyond 4-of-your-major. If opener has made a cue bid, this already indicates better than 7 losers (with 7, or perhaps worse, opener would have merely raised 3-Major to 4-Major). Slam is thus highly likely $(6 + 6 = 12; 24 - 12 = 12$ tricks potential). You should stop below slam only if it is revealed that two key cards are missing or that a suit is clearly unguarded.

If opener makes a cue bid and then signs off in 4-of-your-major, opener is showing exactly 6 losers. When responder bids on despite this attempted sign-off, responder is showing better than 7 losers and that the potential for slam exists.

OPENER	*Responder A*	*Responder B*
♠ K Q 8 6 4	♠ A J 10 3 2	♠ A 9 7 3
♡ K 8	♡ Q 7 6	♡ Q J 6 4
◇ Q J 3	◇ A 6 5	◇ A K 6 2
♣ A 9 5	♣ K 3	♣ 3

1♠ : 3♠		After the jump raise, opener's
4♣ : 4◇		6-loser hand warrants a 4♣ cue
4♠ : ...		followed by a 4♠ signoff over
		4◇. Responder's next move?

Responder A has barely 7 losers (allowing the A-J-10 in spades to counterbalance the weak heart holding) and should pass 4♠. Opener has shown a 6-loser hand, so that with no better than 7 losers, responder should figure that slam will not be a good bet.

Responder B has a sound 6-loser hand. Figuring opener to hold a 6-loser hand also, from the cue bid followed by the sign-off, responder should bid on over 4♠. A further cue bid of 5♣ (showing second round club control) would elicit 5♡ from opener (second round heart control, no second round diamond control) and this should be enough for responder to jump to 6♠.

1♡ : 3NT and 1♠ : 3NT as Balanced Raises

Many partnerships eliminate the 1-Major : 3NT sequence for the balanced 16-18 hand because this removes a lot of bidding space and may inhibit the exploration of slams, particularly minor suit slams. A popular alternative is to treat 1-Major : 3NT as a balanced raise, around the 13-15 point mark (and hence having 7 losers). For example :

♠ A 8	♠ A Q 3	♠ K Q 3	♠ A 7
♡ K Q 6 5	♡ A 10 8 4	♡ A K 9 4	♡ Q J 8 6 2
◊ A 8 4	◊ 8 6 5	◊ 8 7 6 3	◊ K Q 8
♣ J 6 3 2	♣ K Q 3	♣ Q 8	♣ 7 4 2

If partner opens 1♡, each of the above hands is suitable for a response of 3NT as a balanced raise.

After this response, opener with 6-7 losers will sign off in 4-of-the-major but with 5 losers or better, opener will head towards a slam, using either a new suit as a Slam Trial Bid (see page 40) or as a cue bid. Our preference in this area and over limit raises is to use Slam Trials rather than cues. When the high card values for slam are marginal, the degree of fit will be the telling point. Of course, opener may have a slam-going hand where simply asking for aces solves the problems.

Partnerships that use 1-Major : 3NT as balanced, limited raises also frequently use splinter raises.

Splinter Raises

The jumps to 4♣ and 4◊ over a major suit opening are not useful as pre-empts since they are more likely to pre-empt partner and as they bypass 3NT, the best spot for the partnership could be missed.

Many partnerships have harnessed these bids and also the double jump in the other major (1♡ : 3♠ and 1♠ : 4♡) as splinter bids. The splinter shows :

1. The values to go for game. 11 HCP or better is normal.

2. Good support for opener. 4-card or better support is normal.

3. Singleton or void in the suit bid.

4. Normally 6 or 7 losers.

For example :

♠ K J 6 4 3
♡ A 7 3
◊ K J 6 4
♣ 7

After 1♠ by opener, this hand would be worth a 4♣ splinter. The values are definitely too strong for a jump to 4♠. Over 1♡, however, the trump support is inadequate for a splinter.

The splinter raise may be conceived as a short-suit trial for slam. With little or no wastage opposite the short suit, slam can be made on quite modest high card values :

WEST	EAST
♠ 8 7 6 3	♠ A
♡ A Q J 10 6 4	♡ K 9 8 2
◇ 7	◇ A 8 6 4 3
♣ A K	♣ 7 5 4

WEST	EAST
1♡	3♠ (1)
4♣ (2)	4◇ (3)
5♣ (4)	5♠ (5)
5NT (6)	6◇ (7)
7♡ (8)	Pass

(1) Splinter raise, promising a singleton or void in spades, good heart support and enough for game, around the 6-7 loser mark
(2) Cue bid showing the ace of clubs
(3) Cue bid showing the ace of diamonds
(4) Cue bid showing the king of clubs
(5) Cue bid showing the ace of spades or a void in spades
(6) Asking bid in trumps
(7) One top honour in trumps
(8) West can tell that the grand slam requires merely that three spade losers be trumped in dummy. On the actual cards, Roman Key Card Blackwood would work just as well but the above sequence caters also for East holding a void in spades. With a void, East would have some extra high card in the hand to justify the splinter. For example :

♠ —   ♡ K 9 8 2   ◇ A K 6 4 3   ♣ 7 5 4 2

Some partnerships use more sophisticated splinter-showing bids, but these can be gleaned from the relevant system books.

Bidding After a Raise to Game

1♡ : 4♡ or 1♠ : 4♠ – responder has 6-10 HCP, 7 losers :

Opener will generally pass as slam is unlikely but with 5 losers or better plus good controls in the outside suits, opener may either jump to slam or check on aces or make a cue bid.

Imagine the bidding has been 1 ♠ : 4 ♠. What action should opener take now with these hands?

OPENER A	*OPENER B*	*OPENER C*
♠ A Q J 7 6 4	♠ A J 7 6 4 3	♠ A J 7 6 4 3
♡ K Q 6	♡ A Q 6	♡ A Q J
◇ 7 3	◇ 3	◇ 3
♣ K Q	♣ A K 4	♣ K Q J

Opener A should pass 4 ♠. While there are only 5 losers, the controls are poor and responder will not hold three key cards for the 1 ♠ : 4 ♠ raise, as that would be too strong a hand.

Opener B could jump straight to 6 ♠. There are only 5 losers and the controls are excellent. Imagine in each case that responder has :

♠ K 9 8 5 2   ♡ 5 4   ◇ K J 5 4 2   ♣ 2

Opposite Opener A even 4 ♠ might fail while opposite Opener B, 6 ♠ is almost unassailable. It is true that Opener B might contemplate more than just a small slam. A grand slam is feasible but highly unlikely and even if a grand slam were on, there is not enough space for opener to determine that. One does not jeopardise a good small slam for an uncertain grand.

Opener C should use 4NT, Roman Key Card Blackwood preferably. If responder shows only one key card, sign off in 5 ♠ but if two key cards are forthcoming, 6 ♠ should be a reasonable bet.

Raising Opener's Minor

·The principles are similar to those for raising opener's major.

1-Minor : 2-Minor

Responder is showing support for opener, 6-10 points and 8-9 losers. Normally no 4-card major is held and what constitutes support for the minor will depend on the system requirements for opening bids.

1-Minor : 3-Minor

As a limit raise, this shows 10-12 points, sound support for opener's minor with exactly 8 losers, and no 4-card major.

If the 1 ♣ : 3 ♣ and 1 ◇ : 3 ◇ raises are played as game-forcing, they would show 13 or more points, sound support for opener's minor with 7 losers or better, and no major. Naturally the partnership will stipulate whether 1-Minor : 3-Minor is a limit raise or a game-force.

Some systems use "inverted minor raises" where the jump-raise of a minor is essentially pre-emptive and the simple raise of a minor to the two-level is strong (10 points or more) and forcing. In this method, the expectancy for the 1-Minor : 3-Minor sequence would be 6-9 points, good support with 8-9 losers and no major. The strong 1-Minor : 2-Minor raise would promise 10 or more points and the expectancy would be 8 losers or better. Responder's subsequent actions will indicate whether it is only 8 losers (responder will endeavour to sign off below game) or stronger (responder will take strong subsequent action).

1-Minor : 4-Minor

These are generally played as pre-emptive raises, with excellent support, 6-10 HCP and 7 losers, and no 4-card major. They are rarely used since they bypass 3NT which may well be the best spot.

1-Minor : 5-Minor

These are pre-emptive raises based on freak hands with exceptional support. The expectancy is 6-10 HCP plus outstanding support with 6 losers and normally no 4-card major. Responder is also indicating no interest whatsoever in 3NT. For example, bid 5 ◊ over 1 ◊ with :

♠ —   ♡ 7 2   ◊ K 9 8 7 6 4   ♣ Q J 8 6 4

After a minor suit raise, either to the two-level or the three-level, opener's initial problem is whether to try for 3NT or the minor suit game. The **LTC** will indicate whether the 11-trick minor suit game is viable and when slam in a minor is feasible.

Raising Opener's Minimum Rebid

(a) Opener rebids at the one-level (e.g. 1♣ : 1♡, 1♠) :

The principles are similar to those for raising opener's major suit opening. A raise to the two-level should be 6-10 points, 8-9 losers. A raise to the three-level could be used for game-forcing hands but it is more common to treat this as a limit raise. Thus, 1♣ : 1♡, 1♠ : 3♠ would show about 10-12 points and 8 losers while a 4♠ rebid by responder would imply 7 losers and no ambitions for slam. With a stronger hand and with support for opener, responder should use the fourth-suit, for example, 1♣ : 1♡, 1♠ : 2◊ . . . Responder will support spades on the next round and this will be forcing if it is below game, thus suggesting prospects for slam.

If responder wishes to show preference for opener's first suit, again the principles are similar. In the above auction, a rebid of 2♣ by responder would indicate 6-10 points and club support with 8-9 losers, while a jump to 3♣ would generally be played as a limit raise of about 10-12 points and 8 losers. With a game-forcing hand and support for opener's first suit, bid the fourth-suit first (here 2◇) and support the clubs on the next round. Fourth-suit followed by a rebid below game creates a forcing auction.

(b) Opener makes a minimum rebid at the two-level :

(1) Opener rebids in the suit opened (e.g. 1♣ : 1♡, 2♣) :

If you have support for opener's suit (3-card support is adequate), pass with 9 losers or worse and raise to the three-level with 10-12 points and 8 losers as an invitational move. With enough for game and support for opener's suit, you will have to elect between trying for the minor suit game (or slam) and angling for 3NT (bid 3NT direct or bid a new suit forcing in order to check on stoppers). A jump to 4-of-opener's-minor (4♣ in the above example) would be forcing to game and suggesting slam.

(2) Opener rebids in a new suit (e.g. 1♡ : 1♠, 2♣) :

The situation is not forcing in standard methods. With support for the minor and less than 10 points, pass. Likewise, with support for hearts and 9 losers or worse, bid 2♡ as simple preference. With 10-12 points and 8 losers, raise either suit to the 3-level, not forcing but invitational. With enough for game, you can jump to 4♡ or 3NT, bid the fourth-suit or jump to 4-of-opener's-minor as a force to game and a slam suggestion.

(c) Opener's minimum rebid at the two-level over a two-over-one :

(1) Opener rebids in the suit opened (e.g. 1♠ : 2◇, 2♠) :

In standard methods, the situation is not forcing. With tolerance for opener's major and a minimum two-over-one, pass. With support for opener's major and 9 losers, pass. With support for opener's major and 8 losers, raise the major to the three-level as an invitation to game. With 7 losers and support, jump straight to game. With better than 7 losers and prospects for slam, it will depend on the slam methods used by the partnership.

In many modern systems, the two-over-one response creates a game-force. In this case, opener's 2 ♠ rebid obviously cannot be passed and the principles are : with support and a minimum two-over-one, jump to game in opener's major, with support and better values, raise opener's major to the three-level, setting the trump suit, suggesting a slam and invoking the partnership's slam bidding system.

(2) Opener rebids in a new suit :

If opener's second suit is a minor, e.g. 1 ♠ : 2 ♣, 2 ◊ —

Change-of-suit after a two-over-one response is forcing in certain methods. In these methods, with a minimum two-over-one, you may support the minor to the three-level (8 losers, not forcing) or give preference to opener's major at the two-level (8 losers, not forcing). With a stronger responding hand and support for the minor, you may use the fourth-suit (and decide on the best move after opener's rebid) or jump to 4 ◊ as a game-force and slam suggestion. With similar strength and support for the major, jump to game in the major with a bare 7 losers or jump to 3-of-opener's-major with a better hand as a game-force and slam suggestion. Jump rebids after a two-over-one response are forcing to game.

Where the two-over-one response was a game-force, responder's rebids supporting opener's minor to the three-level will be forcing (and will initially suggest a no-trump contract), while supporting opener's major at the two-level would likewise be forcing.

If opener's second suit is hearts (e.g. 1 ♠ : 2 ◊, 2 ♡), it is usual to treat the jump to 4 ♡ as a weaker action than raising to 3 ♡, whether the two-over-one is played as a game-force or as standard.

Responder's actions over opener's strong rebids are dealt with in detail in Chapter 6.

5

Raising Responder's Suit

Major-Suit Raises

1. Opener has 7 losers

Opener will give a single raise (e.g. 1♣ : 1♡, 2♡ or 1◇ : 1♠, 2♠) in virtually any system. The point count expectancy for the single raise is 12-15. On the odd occasion the hand may even contain eight losers. For example, if your system indicates a 1♣ opening on these hands, you would raise a 1♠ response to 2♠ :

♠ K 7 6 4	♠ A K 4 3	♠ A J 7 2
♡ J 8	♡ 6 5 2	♡ Q
◇ A J 2	◇ 8 4 3	◇ J 8 6
♣ A 7 4 3	♣ A Q 7	♣ A J 7 4 3

These situations are the exception and responder will assume the single raise contains the normal minimum opening, 7 losers, or perhaps a bit better rather than perhaps a bit worse.

2. Opener has 6 losers

The jump raise (e.g. 1♣ : 1♡, 3♡ or 1◇ : 1♠, 3♠) indicates a hand of six losers and a high card total of about 15-17. The minimum high card content for the jump raise should be 14. Each of these hands would be suitable :

♠ A 7 6 4	♠ K Q	♠ K 8 7 2
♡ 8	♡ A 8 3 2	♡ A 8 6 5
◇ A J 2	◇ A K 7 3 2	◇ A
♣ K Q 4 3 2	♣ J 6	♣ K J 7 3
Open 1♣	Open 1◇	Open 1♣
Raise 1♠ to 3♠	Raise 1♡ to 3♡	Raise 1♡ to 3♡

Where the opener has a hand of 6 losers but less than 14 high card points, be content to give a single raise. The jump raise of responder's major is similar in concept to the limit raise of opener's major. Just as

1♡ : 3♡ or 1♠ : 3♠ as a limit raise shows 8 losers *and* 10-12 points (with 8 losers and fewer points, raise only to 2♡/2♠), so the jump raise of responder's major is a limit raise, showing 6 losers *and* around 17-18 points, including points for shortages. Just as opener may still try for game after a raise to the two level, so responder can still try for game after a single raise. Each of these hands contains only six losers but should not raise responder beyond the two level :

♠ K Q 6 4	♠ K 9 4 3	♠ K Q 7 2
♡ K 8 7 2	♡ A 7 5 4 2	♡ J 2
◇ 2	◇ 3	◇ K 8 6 5 4
♣ A 7 4 3	♣ K Q 2	♣ A 3
Open 1♣	Open 1♡	Open 1◇
Raise 1♡ to 2♡	Raise 1♠ to 2♠	Raise 1♠ to 2♠

In order to warrant a jump raise with only 11-13 high card points, opener would need to have one less loser. As the high card values diminish, the playing strength needs to increase to justify the same action. Each of these hands would justify opening 1♣ and raising 1♡ to 3♡ :

♠ K Q 6 4	♠ K Q 3	♠ J 2
♡ K 8 7 2	♡ K 9 4 3	♡ K Q 7 3
◇ —	◇ —	◇ A
♣ A 7 4 3 2	♣ A 7 6 5 4 2	♣ K 9 7 5 4 2

3. Opener has 5 losers

The standard action would be to raise responder's major to game (e.g. 1♣ : 1♡, 4♡ or 1◇ : 1♠, 4♠), which indicates a 5 loser hand *and* about 19-21 points, counting shortages. Each of these hands would be suitable to raise responder's 1♠ to 4♠ :

♠ K J 6 4	♠ A K 4 3	♠ A Q 7 2
♡ 8 3	♡ 6 5	♡ 5
◇ K Q J	◇ A 4	◇ K Q J 6
♣ A K Q 3	♣ A Q J 7 6	♣ A J 7 4

Raising responder's major to game should include 16 or more HCP. With 5 losers and less than 16 hcp, a jump raise to the 3-level is sufficient.

♠ A 7 6 4	♠ K 2	♠ K 8 7 2
♡ 8	♡ A 8 3 2	♡ A 8 6 5
◇ K J	◇ A Q 8 7 3 2	◇ —
♣ K Q 6 4 3 2	♣ J	♣ K Q 9 3 2
Open 1 ♣	Open 1 ◇	Open 1 ♣
Raise 1 ♠ to 3 ♠	Raise 1 ♡ to 3 ♡	Raise 1 ♡ to 3 ♡

In order to justify raising responder's major to game with less than 16 high card points, opener should have a hand of 4-4½ losers.

♠ A 2	♠ K Q 4 3	♠ K Q 7 2
♡ K Q 7 2	♡ A 6 5 4 2	♡ 2
◇ 2	◇ —	◇ A K 8 6 5 4 3
♣ A Q 8 7 4 3	♣ K Q 4 2	♣ 3
Open 1 ♣	Open 1 ♡	Open 1 ◇
Raise 1 ♡ to 4 ♡	Raise 1 ♠ to 4 ♠	Raise 1 ♠ to 4 ♠

4. Opener has 4 losers

With a minimum opening (12-15 high card points), raise responder's major to game, as above. With greater high card strength and 4 losers, the system should permit either a splinter raise or a jump-shift, followed by a raise of responder's suit to game. One possible partnership arrangement would be to have the splinter raise to game show a 4-loser hand and about 16-18 high card points, while the jump-shift followed by the raise to game would also show 4 losers but 19 high card points or better. For example :

♠ A Q 6 4	♠ A 8	♠ A K 8 2
♡ K 8	♡ K Q 4 3	♡ K Q 7 3 2
◇ 2	◇ A J	◇ K Q 7
♣ A K 9 4 3 2	♣ A Q 6 5 4	♣ 3
Open 1 ♣. Over	Open 1 ♣. Over	Open 1 ♡. Over
1 ♠, splinter to 4 ◇.	1 ♡, jump shift to	1 ♠, splinter to 4 ♣.
	3 ◇, bid 4 ♡ next.	

It ought to be observed that if your system permits a non-forcing opening bid with a 4-loser hand, you run a considerable risk of missing game. With each of the following hands opposite the ones immediately above, responder should pass the opening bid and a sound game could be missed.

♠ K 7 5 3 2	♠ 9 5 4	♠ Q 7 6 4 3
♡ 4 3 2	♡ J 8 7 6 2	♡ 5 4
◇ 9 8 7	◇ Q 4 3	◇ 9 8
♣ 6 5	♣ 7 2	♣ 10 7 6 4

And responders have been known to pass with better hands than these.

To summarise :

Raise responder's major to 2-level = 7 losers (could be 6 losers if only 11-13 high card points).

Raise responder's major to 3-level = 6 losers (could be 5 losers if only 11-13 high card points).

Raise responder's major to 4-level = 5 losers (could be 4 losers if only 11-15 high card points).

Suppose the bidding has been 1◇ by you and 1♠ from your partner. What action should the opener take next with these hands?

a. ♠ K 9 7 3	b. ♠ K 9 8 2	c. ♠ K 9 6 4	d. ♠ A Q 7 5
♡ Q	♡ A 3	♡ A 3	♡ 10 6
◇ A J 7 4	◇ K Q 8 7 4	◇ A K 8 7 3	◇ A K J 6 2
♣ K 9 7 2	♣ 9 2	♣ J 2	♣ K 9

Answers :

(a) 7 losers. Raise to 2♠.

(b) 6 losers but only 12 HCP. Raise to 2♠ only.

(c) 6 losers. 15 HCP, 17 total points. Raise to 3♠.

(d) 5 losers, 17 HCP, 19 total points. Raise to 4♠. This is, in fact, the opening hand of the deal which appears on page 9.

Subsequent Bidding After a Major Raise

Responder's action after opener's raise to the 2-level (6-7 losers)

With 9 losers or more :	Pass
With 8 losers	: Invite game
With 7 losers	: Bid game
With 6 losers	: Consider slam; make a slam try

With 5 losers or fewer :   Explore slam; bid slam unless two key
cards are missing

(a) Responder has 9 losers or worse

Where the responder has 9 losers, game prospects are too remote.
With opener's 7 losers opposite 9 losers, 8 tricks will be the limit and
opposite 8 losers, the expectancy is only 9 tricks. Thus a move beyond
the 2-level will only jeopardise a decent partscore.

WEST	EAST	WEST	EAST
♠ K J 7 2	♠ A 8 6 5	1♣	1♠
♡ K 7	♡ J 5 4	2♠	Pass
◇ Q 10 3	◇ J 7 2		
♣ A 9 8 3	♣ K Q 2		

Despite the 11 points, East has 9 losers and should pass 2♠. Game is
possible but is highly unlikely. 4♠ requires a 3-2 break in spades, the
spade finesse, the heart finesse and no diamond ruff. All in all, less than
a 20% chance. If East were to push on, 2NT is the move, but best is for
East to pass 2♠. You will have your triumph when 3♠ proves to be too
high on slightly unlucky days.

(b) Responder has 8 losers

Where responder has 8 losers, it is worth exploring game chances
after a raise to 2-major, since opener may have 6 losers but have less
than 14 high card points. The best means will usually be a Trial Bid as
illustrated in the previous chapter. For example –

WEST	EAST	WEST	EAST
♠ K J 7 2	♠ A 9 6 4 3	1♣	1♠
♡ K 7	♡ 8 6 5 2	2♠	3♡ (1)
◇ Q 10 2	◇ A J	4♠	Pass
♣ A 9 8 3	♣ 7 4		(1) Long suit trial bid

With 8 losers and good controls, East is worth a try for game. On a
club lead, declarer has chances in each of the other suits to limit the
losers. Without a club lead, declarer can benefit from this respite by
setting up a diamond winner to discard a club loser.

(c) Responder has 7 losers

WEST	EAST	WEST	EAST
♠ K J 7 2	♠ A 9 8 6 4 3	1♣	1♠
♡ K 7	♡ Q J 3 2	2♠	4♠
◇ Q 10 3	◇ 6 5	Pass	
♣ A 9 8 3	♣ 4		

Here East has only 7 losers, 7 + 7 = 14. 24 − 14 = 10 tricks potential. Contrast this with Hand (a) above. On (a), East had 11 HCP and it was right to pass 2♠. On (c) East has 7 HCP and it is right to jump straight to 4♠. Quite a dramatic example that points are not everything.

(d) Responder has better than 7 losers

Suppose the bidding has been 1♣ : 1♠, 2♠ . . . What action should responder now take with –

♠ A Q 6 5 4   ♡ A J 8 3 2   ◇ A J   ♣ 4 ?

The hand has 5 losers. 5 + 7 = 12. 24 − 12 = 12 tricks potential, so that responder should make a move towards slam.

Slam will almost certainly hinge on the heart position. If opener has three low hearts, slam is unlikely but with a good fit in hearts, slam is almost certain. Responder's best shot is a long suit trial bid in hearts. If it receives a negative reaction, 4♠ is enough, or at most, a slam suggestion via a cue bid of 4◇. For example –

WEST	EAST	WEST	EAST
♠ K 9 7 2	♠ A Q 6 5 4	1♣	1♠
♡ 6 5 4	♡ A J 8 3 2	2♠	3♡ – Trial bid
◇ K Q	◇ A J	3♠	4◇ – Cue bid
♣ K Q 7 6	♣ 4	4♠	Pass

On the other hand, if the 3♡ receives an enthusiastic reaction, East bids on to the slam. For example –

WEST	EAST	WEST	EAST
♠ K J 7 2	♠ A Q 6 5 4	1♣	1♠
♡ K 7	♡ A J 8 3 2	2♠	3♡
◇ Q 10 3	◇ A J	4♠	6♠
♣ A 9 8 3	♣ 4	Pass	

Here too, West has 13 points and 7 losers, but what a difference! In reply to the 3♡ trial bid, West accepts the invitation and jumps to game. Always accept a trial bid with only one loser in the trial suit. East could check on the aces and kings held, but even if West held the king of diamonds instead of the queen, a grand slam is only a fair bet since the heart suit has to be brought in. Reaching 6♠ (and making thirteen tricks if possible) will give you a fine result in most games anyway.

Raising Responder In Other Systems :

Where your system diverges from standard practice, you may need to adjust the loser count in accordance with the dictates of the system. This is particularly so if the system advocates regularly light opening bids. The most prevalent case would be the Precision System where opening bids on 11 points are commonplace. In Precision, the guidelines would be that auctions such as 1◇ : 1♠, 2♠ would show 7-8 losers (rather than the 6-7 losers associated with that raise in standard methods) while sequences like 1◇ : 1♠, 3♠ would be based on a 6-loser hand but with only 13-15 HCP, since the failure to open 1♣ denies 16 HCP in Precision.

Responder's action after opener's raise to the 3-level

For example, after 1♣ : 1♡, 3♡ . . . or 1◇ : 1♠, 3♠ . . . where opener is expected to have 16-18 points and 6 losers :

> With 9 losers or worse : Pass
> (6 + 9 = 15; 24 − 15 = 9 tricks potential)

> With 7 or 8 losers : Bid game
> (8 + 6 = 14, 24 − 14 = 10. 7 + 6 = 13; 24 − 13 = 11 tricks potential. Slam is unlikely, but game will be a good bet.)

> With 6 losers or fewer : Explore for slam
> (6 + 6 = 12; 24 − 12 = 12 tricks potential)

Responder's action after opener's raise to game

For example, after 1♣ : 1♡, 4♡ . . . or 1◇ : 1♠, 4♠ . . . where opener has good support for responder and an expectancy of 5 losers :

> With 8 losers or worse : Pass
> (8 + 5 = 13; 24 − 13 = 11. Slam is unlikely.)

With 7 losers or better : Explore slam
(7 + 5 = 12; 24 − 12 = 12 tricks potential)

Where opener has good support and a maximum opening

With 3 losers or fewer, opener should not start with a droppable opening bid, but in standard methods, hands around the 20-point mark, about 4-5 losers, are possible. There are two ways that the opener can indicate a hand with great support and massive playing strength, a hand too strong even for the immediate raise to game (showing 5 losers) :

(1) Jump-shift first and support responder on the next round. The jump-shift itself indicates 19 points or more and will be based on a 4-loser hand.

(2) Use a splinter bid. Opener can splinter after a 1-level response just as responder can (see pages 45-46). Splinters by opener are commonly used in seasoned partnerships where opener has a hand of 5 losers or better *plus* strong support. For example :

WEST	EAST	WEST	EAST	WEST	EAST
1♦	1♡	1♡	1♠	1♣	1♠
3♠ . . .		4♣ . . .		4♦ . . .	

Heart support, enough for game, 4-5 losers, singleton or void in spades.	Spade support, enough for game, 4-5 losers, singleton or void in clubs.	Spade support, enough for game, 4-5 losers, singleton or void in diamonds.

After a splinter raise, responder should be enthusiastic about slam prospects with 8 losers if there is little or no high card strength wasted opposite the short suit. With 7 losers or better, responder should head for a slam even if there is wasted strength opposite the shortage. With no interest in slam, responder will sign off in game. With slam chances, responder can cue bid or use 4NT. For example :

WEST	EAST	WEST	EAST
♠ A Q 7 5	♠ K 9 8 3 2	♠ Q J 7 5	♠ K 9 8 3 2
♡ K 4 3	♡ J 6 5	♡ K Q J	♡ 9 8 5 2
♦ A K Q 9 3	♦ 7	♦ A K Q 9 3	♦ 7
♣ 6	♣ Q J 5 2	♣ 6	♣ A Q 3

WEST	EAST
1◇	1♠
4♣	4♠
Pass	

WEST	EAST
1◇	1♠
4♣	4NT
5◇ (1)	5♠

(1) 1 or 4 key cards, clearly 1

WEST	EAST
♠ A Q 7 5	♠ K 9 8 3 2
♡ K 4 3	♡ A 8 6
◇ A K Q 9 3	◇ 7
♣ 6	♣ 9 8 5 2

WEST	EAST
♠ A 7 5 4	♠ K Q 8 3 2
♡ A 4 3	♡ 9 8 5 2
◇ A K Q 4 3	◇ 7
♣ 6	♣ A 5 2

WEST	EAST
1◇	1♠
4♣	4NT
5♠ (1)	6♠
Pass	

WEST	EAST
1◇	1♠
4♣	4NT
5♣ (1)	6♠
Pass	

(1) 2 key cards + trump queen

(1) 0 or 3 key cards

WEST	EAST
♠ A 9 7 5	♠ K Q 8 6 2
♡ K Q 6	♡ A 3 2
◇ A K Q 6 5	◇ 7
♣ 7	♣ A 6 4 3

WEST	EAST
♠ A J 5 4	♠ K Q 8 6 2
♡ A J 10	♡ 6 4 2
◇ K Q J 9 7 4	◇ A 2
♣ —	♣ 8 4 3

WEST	EAST
1◇	1♠
4♣	4NT
5♡	5NT
6♡	7♠
Pass	

WEST	EAST
1◇	1♠
4♣	4◇ (1)
5NT (2)	6♡ (3)
7♠	Pass

(1) Cue bid, showing the ace
(2) Trump asking bid
(3) Two top trumps

After 1♣ : 1◇ — Opener Supports Diamonds

1♣ : 1◇
2◇ — Diamond support with 13-15 points, 6-7 losers

1♣ : 1◇
3◇ — Diamond support with 16-18 points, 5-6 losers

Standard systems do not provide a satisfactory solution for opener's 4-loser hands with diamond support. Some partnerships utilise a specific two-opening for such hands, while others use a splinter raise (for example, 1♣ : 1◇, 3♡ . . . or 1♣ : 1◇, 3♠ . . .) to cater for this problem hand.

♠ 7   If you open 1♣ and partner responds 1◇,
♡ A 8 2   the hand is too strong for 3◇. In view of the
◇ A Q 6 4   spades, 3NT is out and a jump-shift to 2♡
♣ A K Q 5 2   runs the risk of hearts being raised. A splinter
                           raise of 3♠ is ideal.

A jump-shift into a lower-ranking suit is reasonably safe since you can always revert to the higher suit, but a jump-shift into a higher suit does not have this safety mechanism.

Opener Raises a 2-Minor Response

1. Standard Style

The 2-level response in standard methods shows 10 or more points and opener should place responder with 8 losers or better.

Raise to 3-level (e.g. 1♡ : 2♣, 3♣) = Support and 6-7 losers

Jump-raise to 4-level (e.g. 1♡ : 2♣, 4♣) = Support and 5 losers or better. Forcing to game and suggesting slam possibilities.

It can be logically deduced that auctions such as 1♡ : 2♣, 4♣ . . . or 1♡ : 2◇, 4◇ . . . shows five losers or better for opener. Given that these sequences are forcing to game and that opener can count on no better than 8 losers with responder, opener needs a 5-loser hand so that the **LTC** will work out for the 5-minor game of 11 tricks :

24 − ? = 11 tricks . . . the answer here is 13.
8 + ? = 13 . . . and here the answer is 5 which is what opener needs.

If opener held 6 losers, the **LTC** formula would work out as 6 + 8 = 14; 24 − 14 = 10 tricks, but this is not enough for game in a minor, of course.

It is not attractive to jump raise a minor to game since it precludes partner's use of 4NT and eliminates any cue bidding. In most sequences, even a non-jump raise of 4-of-a-minor is better played as forcing and slam-going than as invitational. Otherwise, how do you explore slams?

After opener's raise of responder's minor to the 3-level

For example, after 1♠ : 2♣, 3♦ : ? where opener has 6-7 losers, if responder has a no-trump-type hand, responder can bid 3NT or bid a stopper at the 3-level. If responder intends to play in the minor suit :

With 8 losers : Pass — game at the 5-level will be a poor bet with 8 losers opposite 6-7 losers, since the potential in your trump suit will be only 9 or 10 tricks. For example, you should pass 3♣ in the above auction with :

$$\spadesuit \; Q\,2 \qquad \heartsuit \; J\,7\,2 \qquad \diamondsuit \; 7\,5\,4 \qquad \clubsuit \; A\,Q\,J\,8\,2$$

With 7 losers : Game is not certain, but it is possible, so keep bidding. Bid a stopper at the 3-level, then revert to four of your minor if 3NT is not suitable. Suppose the bidding has been 1♠ : 2♣, 3♣ : ? What is your next action on these cards :

$$\spadesuit \; 7 \qquad \heartsuit \; 6\,4\,2 \qquad \diamondsuit \; K\,J\,8\,3 \qquad \clubsuit \; A\,Q\,J\,6\,5$$

Your best bet is to bid 3♦, to show that stopper. If opener rebids 3NT or 4♣, you should pass, while if opener rebids 3♠, denying a stopper in hearts but showing five good spades, remove this to 4♣, not forcing.

With 6 losers or better : Game is a good bet and slam is possible. You may show a stopper at the 3-level for 3NT or start a cue-bidding auction at the 4-level or simply ask for aces.

Example Hands

WEST	EAST	WEST	EAST
♠ K8	♠ A 7 3	1♡	2◇
♡ A J 5 3 2	♡ 6	3◇	4♣ (1)
◇ Q J 10 2	◇ A K 9 8 6 4	4♡ (1)	4♠ (1)
♣ Q 8	♣ A 7 6	5◇ (2)	6◇ (3)
		Pass	

(1) Cue bid showing first round control
(2) With 7 losers rather than 6 and no second round club control, West signs off in 5◇ rather than cue bid 5♠ to show the king
(3) East has enough to bid the small slam anyway.

WEST	EAST	WEST	EAST
♠ K 8	♠ A 3	1♡	2♢
♡ A J 5 3 2	♡ 6	3♢	4♣ (1)
♢ Q J 10 2	♢ A K 9 8 6 4 3	4♡ (1)	4♠ (1)
♣ K 8	♣ A 7 6	5♣ (2)	5♡ (2)
		5♠ (2)	7♢ (3)
		Pass	

(1) Cue bid showing first round control of the suit bid
(2) Cue bid showing second round control of the suit bid
(3) If opener's 5♠ cue bid happened to be a singleton and opener did not have the king of hearts, on a hand such as this :

♠ 2   ♡ A J 5 3 2   ♢ Q J 10 2   ♣ K J 5

declarer in 7♢ would aim to set up the fifth heart to discard the club loser, and if that failed, the club finesse would be the last resort.

After opener gives a jump raise to 4-minor

For example, after 1♡ : 2♣, 4♣ . . . or 1♠ : 2♢, 4♢ . . . where opener has good support for responder and 5 losers or better :

With 8 losers : Responder may cue bid, but should not bid beyond the 5-level in the agreed minor, since the values for slam are by no means certain (8 + 5 = 13; 24 − 13 = 11). With no convenient cue bid, responder would simply raise to 5 of the minor to confirm a bare 8-loser hand. If responder cue bids and then rebids 5-of-the-agreed minor, that tends to show no control in the missing suit rather than a modest hand.

With 7 losers or better : Responder has the values for slam. Responder may cue bid or ask for aces and should push on to slam unless it becomes evident that there are two certain or two likely losers.

WEST	EAST	WEST	EAST
♠ 9 2	♠ J 8 7	♠ K Q	♠ J 8 7
♡ A K Q 7 2	♡ 4	♡ A Q 7 3 2	♡ 4
♢ Q 4	♢ A K 5	♢ J 4	♢ A K 5
♣ K Q J 7	♣ A 9 8 6 4 2	♣ K Q J 7	♣ A 9 8 6 4 2

WEST	EAST		WEST	EAST
1♡	2♣		1♡	2♣
4♣	4◇ (1)		4♣	4◇ (1)
4♡ (1)	5♣ (2)		4♡ (1)	5♣ (2)
Pass (3)			6♣ (3)	Pass

(1) Cue Bid   (1) Cue bid
(2) Denies spade control   (2) Worried about the spades
(3) Also no control of spades   (3) Having the spade control

WEST	EAST		WEST	EAST
♠ A 7	♠ K 8 2		♠ A 7	♠ 9 6 2
♡ A 9 7 6 2	♡ 5		♡ K Q J 5 2	♡ 7
◇ A J	♡ K Q 3		◇ K Q	◇ A 7 4
♣ K J 5 4	♣ A Q 9 7 3 2		♣ Q J 10 3	♣ A K 8 6 4 2

WEST	EAST		WEST	EAST
1♡	2♣		1♡	2♣
4♣	4NT		4♣	4◇ (1)
5◇ (1)	5NT		4♠ (1)	6♣ (2)
6♣ (2)	7♣		Pass	
Pass				

(1) 1 or 4 key cards for clubs
(2) No extra kings. If West shows
the ♡K, East bids 7NT.

(1) Cue bid
(2) East knows that West has the
  ♠ A but not the ♡ A, so that 7♣
is out of the question.

2. Modern Methods — 2-Over-1 Game Force

The above guidelines apply, as in standard methods, except that the raise to 3-of-responder's-minor will be forcing because of the forcing nature of the 2-over-1 response. The subsequent bidding after a raise of responder's minor to the 3-level or to the 4-level is the same as that given above.

3. Splinters After a 2-Minor Response

Since a change of suit after a 2-over-1 response is played as forcing in certain methods, a jump-shift is used by some partnerships not to show a huge hand but to show a shortage in the suit bid, support for responder's major and a count of 5 losers or better (enough for game). Because slam bidding is severely condensed for the minor suits (due to the unavailability of the 5-level), using splinters after a 2-minor response works very well in enabling responder to judge whether the values held are working or are duplication. Except for the ace, the less high card strength opposite the shortage the better the prospects for slam.

WEST	EAST	WEST	EAST
♠ A Q 7 6 2	♠ K 3	♠ 7	♠ A 5 4 2
♡ A Q 4	♡ K 7	♡ A Q 8 6 5	♡ K 4
◇ K J 10 2	◇ A Q 9 7 4	◇ K 8 6 4 3	◇ A Q 9 5 2
♣ 8	♣ A 7 5 2	♣ A 9	♣ K 9

WEST	EAST	WEST	EAST
1♠	2◇	1♡	2◇
4♣ (1)	4NT	3♠ (1)	4NT
5♣ (2)	7◇	5♣ (2)	7◇
Pass		Pass	

(1) Splinter, short in clubs   (1) Splinter, short in spades
(2) 0 or 3 key cards for diamonds   (2) 0 or 3 key cards

After 1♠ : 2♡ . . .

Responder has shown *five* or more hearts, 10 or more points and the loser expectancy is 8 losers or better. Where opener has support for hearts, the options in standard methods are :

1♠ : 2♡
3♡ — Opener has 7 losers, heart support, minimum opening.

1♠ : 2♡
4♡ — Opener has 6 losers, heart support, better than a minimum opening.

1♠ : 2♡
4♣ or 4◇ — These are splinters with heart support, singleton or void in the suit bid and a hand of 5 losers or better. Some partnerships use the splinters on hands with 6 losers or better and the raise to 4♡ as a 6-loser hand with no shortage (5-3-3-2 or 5-4-2-2 patterns).

Standard methods fare badly when opener has five spades, four hearts, better than 6 losers but no singleton or void. Suppose you picked up :

♠ A Q J 4 3   ♡ K 9 6 2   ◇ A K   ♣ 4 3

What rebid would you find after 1♠ : 2♡? Some players would manufacture a 3◇ rebid, an advance cue bid, and support the hearts later. Aside from the difficulties that flow from such an approach, what would you rebid after 1♠ : 2♡ with no outside ace, such as :

♠ A K J 4 3   ♡ K Q 8 6   ◇ K 2   ♣ 4 3

To try to cope with problems like these, some pairs adopt a different approach to raises of the 2♡ response :

1♠ : 2♡
4♡ — Opener has a minimum hand, support for hearts, 7 losers.

1♠ : 2♡
3♡ — Opener has support for hearts, better than a minimum, 6 losers or better. The raise to 3♡ is thus forcing to game and suggests slam. The splinter bids of 4♣ and 4◇ are still available and thus 3♡ tends to suggest a flatter hand and invites partner to start cue bidding. With this approach, you reach a light game on the odd occasion (7 losers opposite 8) but the slam area does not suffer.

Partnerships that use a 2-over-1 game-force system adopt the same approach, with the raise to 4♡ indicating a minimum opening and the raise to 3♡ promising additional values and inviting a cue bid.

Other partnerships, in an endeavour to deal with these kinds of problems, turn to Precision and other big club systems which allow more room to explore the big hands, provided that the opponents are considerate enough to desist from interfering.

Quiz For Chapters 4 & 5

1. Partner has opened 1♠. How many losers are shown by responder in each of these auctions?

a. 1♠ : 3♠ limit raise
b. 1♠ : 3♠ pre-emptive raise
c. 1♠ : 3♠ game-force
d.   Pass
    1♠ : 3♠ — standard methods

2. Partner has opened 1♠. What is your response with :

a. ♠ K 8 6 4   b. ♠ A 9 8 2   c. ♠ A 9 8 2   d. ♠ A 9 8 6
   ♡ 7   ♡ K 4 3   ♡ K 4 3   ♡ K Q 4
   ◇ A 8 6 5 4 2   ◇ Q 7 6   ◇ Q J 9 8   ◇ K J 4 3 2
   ♣ 5 4   ♣ J 9 8   ♣ 7 6   ♣ 6

3. You and your partner are using Long Suit Trials. What is your rebid as responder on these hands after 1♠ : 2♠, 3◇?

a. ♠ J 7 3 2
   ♡ 7 4
   ◇ K Q J 8
   ♣ 4 3 2

b. ♠ J 7 3 2
   ♡ 7 4
   ◇ 8 4 3
   ♣ K Q J 8

c. ♠ Q J 4 2
   ♡ 8 5 3 2
   ◇ 7
   ♣ K 6 4 3

d. ♠ Q 7 5 4
   ♡ J 8 6 2
   ◇ —
   ♣ J 7 6 4 3

4. You opened 1♣ and partner responded 1♠. What is your rebid?

a. ♠ A K 4 3
   ♡ 7
   ◇ A 9 4
   ♣ A Q 8 7 3

b. ♠ K Q 7 3
   ♡ 4
   ◇ K 2
   ♣ A K 8 6 4 2

c. ♠ A 8 6 4
   ♡ 7 5 2
   ◇ 8
   ♣ A K J 9 4

d. ♠ J 7 6 4
   ♡ A K 2
   ◇ 8
   ♣ A Q 9 6 3

5. The bidding has been 1♠ : 2♣, 3♣. What is your rebid as responder on these hands?

a. ♠ 6
   ♡ 7 4 3
   ◇ A Q 3
   ♣ A J 7 6 4 2

b. ♠ J 8 6
   ♡ 9 4
   ◇ K Q 8 2
   ♣ A Q 5 4

c. ♠ 6
   ♡ K Q 4 2
   ◇ K 8
   ♣ A K 9 7 6 2

d. ♠ K 2
   ♡ A Q 3
   ◇ 7 3
   ♣ A K 7 6 3 2

Answers

1. a. 8 losers   b. 8 losers   c. 7 losers or better   d. 8 losers

2. a. 4♠ – 7 losers   b. 2♠ – 9½ losers   c. 3♠ if using limit raises; if not, bid 2◇ and support spades later, since 10 HCP and 8 losers is too good to raise just to 2♠   d. 3♠ if forcing *or* 4♣ as a splinter raise (best action if available) *or* 2◇ and support spades later with a forcing bid.

3. a. 4♠ — only 1 loser in the trial suit   b. 3♠ — 3 losers in the trial suit   c. 4♠ — only 1 loser in the trial suit   d. 4♠ — no losers in the trial suit

4. a. 4♠ (or 4♡ splinter)   b. 4♠ (or 4♡ splinter)   c. 2♠   d. 3♠

5. a. 3◇, a stopper bid, angling for 3NT if partner has the hearts stopped   b. 4♠, as partner will have five spades   c. 4NT, heading for a small slam or a grand slam   d. 4♣, forcing, aiming for a slam but concerned about the diamonds. Partner is asked to start cue bidding.

6
Opener's Strong Actions

(1) Opener's Reverse

Opener's reverse is a 2-level bid in a suit higher ranking than the suit opened. Each of the following rebids by opener constitutes a reverse :

1♣	:	1♠		1◇	:	2♣		1◇	:	1♠		1♣	:	1♡
2♡	...			2♠	...			2♡	...			2◇	...	

The reverse shows a hand which is not balanced and in which the lower ranking suit is the longer. One does not reverse with suits of equal length. In standard systems, the reverse shows around 16-17 points or more. These hands are typically worth a reverse :

♠ A 7	♠ 4	♠ A 65	♠ A 3
♡ A Q 8 2	♡ K Q J	♡ A K 9 2	♡ A J 5 2
◇ A K 7 6 5	◇ K Q J 2	◇ 8	◇ A Q J 8 6 2
♣ 4 3	♣ A 8 7 6 5	♣ A Q J 5 3	♣ 9

In terms of the **LTC**, a reverse should hold :

16 HCP or better (in which case the loser count might be 6), *or, if less than 16 HCP*, 5 losers or better.

Even though these hands contain fewer than 16 HCP, one should open 1◇ and reverse with 2♡ over a response of 1♠, 1NT or 2♣ :

♠ 3 2	♠ 4	♠ 4	♠ 7
♡ A Q 8 3	♡ A Q 9 8	♡ A Q J 10	♡ K Q 8 7 4
◇ A K Q 6 4	◇ A K J 8 5 3	◇ K Q J 9 7 4	◇ A K 9 4 3 2
♣ 4 3	♣ 3 2	♣ 9 6	♣ 2

By contrast, these hands are too weak for a 1◇ opening, 2♡ reverse :

(a) ♠ A J	(b) ♠ K Q	(c) ♠ A Q
♡ K J 5 2	♡ A 7 3 2	♡ K J 7 5 3
◇ A 9 7 3 2	◇ K 8 6 4 3 2	◇ J 8 6 4 3 2
♣ Q 3	♣ Q	♣ —

(a) Either open a strong 1NT or after opening 1◇, rebid 1NT over 1♠. Do not rebid 2♡ — only 15 HCP, 7 losers, minimum hand.

(b) After opening 1◇, rebid 2◇ over a response of 1♠, 1NT or 2♣. Do not rebid 2♡ with only 14 HCP and 6 losers. Below 16 HCP, you need a 5-loser or better hand to justify a reverse.

(c) Open 1♡ and rebid 2◇ rather than open 1◇ and reverse with 2♡. This hand has only 11 HCP and 6 losers and the long suits are too weak to justify a reverse. However, it is not appealing to open 1◇ and rebid 2◇, which could lose the heart suit entirely. Rather lie about the shape than risk losing a 5-card major.

Responder to the reverse will treat opener's hand as a 5-loser hand when supporting either of opener's suits. The most common treatment after a reverse is for responder to show a 6-8 point hand via one of the weak rebids (support opener's second suit, show preference for opener's first suit, rebid responder's suit or rebid 2NT) or to bid the fourth suit or make a jump rebid to show hands with 9 or more points. Both of these latter strong bids are forcing to game.

If opener hears a weak rebid by responder, opener will usually pass with a normal 16-18 point, 5 loser hand, but with 19 points or more or with a 4-loser hand, opener should make one more move towards game.

WEST	EAST	WEST	EAST
♠ 7	♠ K 9 8 5 2	♠ 7	♠ A 9 8 5 2
♡ K Q J 2	♡ 8 7	♡ K Q J 2	♡ 7 6
◇ A 8 3	◇ Q 7 5	◇ A 8	◇ 9 5 4
♣ A Q 8 7 5	♣ J 3 2	♣ A Q 8 7 5 4	♣ K 3 2

WEST	EAST	WEST	EAST
1♣	1♠	1♣	1♠
2♡	3♣	2♡	3♣
Pass		4♣ (1)	5♣ (2)
		Pass	

(1) With only 4 losers, opener makes one more try. 3◇ as a stopper probe was also possible, but the likely need to set up heart tricks makes no-trumps less attractive.

(2) Given that opener should have a 4-loser hand for bidding again after East's sign-off, East can count on covering two of those four losers.

Cover Cards

The concept of "cover cards" was devised by George Rosenkranz as part of his Romex System but is invaluable in any system. A cover card is a card that eliminates a loser in partner's hand. Your high cards are "working" when they eliminate losers, when they operate as cover cards. Your high cards are not working, there is *duplication of values*, when your high cards do not eliminate losers in partner's hand, when they do not "cover" the losers. As an example :

OPENER	Responder A	Responder B
♠ 2	♠ A 5 4	♠ K Q J
♡ A K Q J	♡ 4 3 2	♡ 4 3 2
◇ A K Q J 10 9 8	◇ 4 3 2	◇ 4 3 2
♣ 2	♣ A 5 4 3	♣ K Q J 3

Opposite Responder A, the two hands can produce a grand slam. Opposite Responder B, the limit is eleven tricks, even though Responder B has more points. Responder A's two aces cover opener's losers, while Responder B's values do not. Responder B's black suits are an example of extreme duplication.

Where partner is known to hold a long strong suit *or* partner's shape is pretty well known (such as after a reverse, where opener is known to be at least 5-4 in the suits bid), then if you know how many losers partner holds, you can calculate the trick-taking potential of the two hands very simply :

> *Deduct your cover cards from partner's losers.*
> *Deduct the answer from 13. The answer is the tricks expected.*

On the example above, opener has two losers. Responder A has two cover cards. 2 – 0 = 0. Zero losers means 13 winners. Responder B had no cover cards. 2 – 0 = 2. 13 – 2 = 11 tricks. Two losers = eleven winners.

What Counts as a Cover Card?

In partner's known long suit or suits, each ace, king or queen counts as a cover card. Outside partner's known long suits, the lower the honour, the less valuable it is as a cover card. An outside ace is almost always a cover card (it may not be when partner is void in that suit), a king might cover a loser but an outside suit headed by the queen or jack is of limited value for partner. A-K probably covers two losers and K-Q will cover one loser except if partner has a singleton in that suit. The more you know about partner's shape, the better will be your appreciation of the cover cards held.

Where you are very strong in the outside suits, you can often tell that all of partner's outside losers are covered. For example, if you know that partner has 5 diamonds-4 hearts, then you know that there are no losers outside those suits if you hold ♠ A-K-♣ A-K or ♠ A-K-Q-♣ A or ♠ A-♣ A-K-Q. No matter how partner's black suits are distributed, your black winners will cover them all.

Reverting to an earlier example where a reversing opener had 4 losers :

OPENER	Responder A	Responder B
♠ 7	♠ A 9 8 5 2	♠ K J 8 5 2
♡ K Q J 2	♡ 7 6	♡ 7 6
◇ A 8	◇ 9 5 4	◇ 9 5 4
♣ A Q 8 7 5 4	♣ K 3 2	♣ K 3 2

Opener	Responder
1♣	1♠
2♡	3♣
4♣	?

Given that opener has indicated a 4-loser hand, Responder A should accept the invitation as two of opener's four losers are covered. Responder B should pass 4♠, since it is likely that only the king of clubs is useful. The spade holding may cover a loser but it is not likely. On the marked diamond lead, 5♣ is almost hopeless opposite Responder B.

The concept of cover cards is most useful when partner has a long, strong suit or partner has a known two-suiter with the suit lengths known. In such cases, it is usually simpler to use cover cards since the shape of the dummy hand will often not be as relevant as the number of cover cards held. For example, after opener's reverse (opener has a 5-loser hand), if a trump fit has been located, slam prospects should be considered if responder has 7 losers ($7+5=12$; $24-12=12$ tricks potential) or if responder has 4 cover cards (5 losers – 4 cover cards = 1 loser = 12 winners) :

OPENER	Responder A	Responder B	Responder C
♠ 3 2	♠ A K 6 5	♠ K Q J 5	♠ A K 6
♡ A Q 6 5	♡ K 7	♡ K 7	♡ K 7 3
◇ K Q J 7 4	◇ A 8 5 2	◇ A 8 5 2	◇ A 8 5 2
♣ A 8	♣ 6 4 2	♣ J 6 4	♣ 6 4 2

The diamond fit and the high card content is the same in each case. Responders A and B both have 7 losers, but 6◇ is a good bet only opposite A. Responder A covers 4 losers but Responder B covers only 3 losers (and the almost certain club lead will defeat 6 ◇). Responder C has 8 losers and yet 6 ◇ is still virtually laydown, because Responder C *is able to cover 4 losers*. The **LTC** is not the determining factor here.

(2) Opener's Jump Rebids

Until a trump fit has been located, the **LTC** does not operate. However, opener's strength can be gauged from the rebid chosen and hence an estimate can be made of opener's losers.

After a 1-level reply, opener's rebids in the same suit are almost always based on a 6-card or longer suit. The ranges are :

Simple rebid (e.g. 1◇ : 1♡, 2◇) = 12-15 points, 6-7 losers

7 losers :   ♠ K Q   ♡ K 3   ◇ A 9 6 5 4 2   ♣ 7 4 3

6 losers :   ♠ A K 4   ♡ 7 3   ◇ A Q 8 6 5 4   ♣ 4 3

Jump rebid (e.g. 1◇ : 1♡, 3◇) = 16-18 points, 5-6 losers

6 losers :   ♠ A 8 3   ♡ A J   ◇ K Q J 9 8 6   ♣ J 8

5 losers :   ♠ J 4 2   ♡ 4   ◇ A K Q 8 7 6   ♣ A Q 8

Opener may make a jump-rebid in the suit opened with fewer than 16 high card points, but if so, the hand should contain only 5 losers, not 6. The extra playing trick is the compensation for the lower high card values. After 1◇ : 1♡, it would be too timid to rebid merely 2◇ on these hands :

5 losers :   ♠ 2   ♡ 3 2   ◇ A K 9 8 6 4 3   ♣ A Q 8

5 losers :   ♠ A   ♡ 7 4   ◇ A K Q J 8 6   ♣ 8 6 4 3

Where opener's suit is a major, opener's rebids follow the same pattern :

Minimum rebid (e.g. 1♡ : 1♠, 2♡) = Minimum opening, 6-7 losers

Jump rebid (e.g. 1♡ : 1♠, 3♡) = Strong opening, 5-6 losers

Game rebid (e.g. 1♡ : 1♠, 4♡) = Maximum opening, 4 losers

For example :

♠ 4   ♡ K Q J 10 8 3 2   ◇ K Q J   ♣ A 3

After 1♡ : 1♠, a rebid of 3♡ would not do justice to this 4-loser hand. Rebid 4♡.

After opener's jump rebid (e.g. 1♣ : 1◇, 3♣ *or* 1♡ : 1♠, 3♡), if responder has a fit for opener's suit, responder should investigate slam with 7 losers or better or with 4 cover cards or better. After opener's game rebid (e.g. 1♡ : 1♠, 4♡), responder with support for opener's suit should investigate slam chances if holding 8 losers or better or 3 cover cards or better.

In standard methods, there is no rebid which copes with opener holding a long, single-suited minor and 4 losers. Sequences like 1♣ : 1♠, 3♣ *or* 1◇ : 1♠, 3◇ are not forcing and one cannot afford a droppable bid with a 4-loser hand, facing a responder with 6 points at least. Players who do open 1♣ or 1◇ on such hands try to catch up later via a fake jump-shift or a desperation bash at 3NT.

Acol Two Openings, showing 8-9 playing tricks, (see later in this chapter) cope with such hands far more efficiently. A standard system which regularly opens 4-loser hands with a droppable 1-opening is less than satisfactory, since one can easily be passed out at the 1-level and miss a game. A forcing 1♣ opening or a strong 1♣ opening or the Benjamin Twos structure can cope far more efficiently in this area.

WEST	EAST	Many pairs would miss the
♠ A Q J 10 4	♠ 7	superb 4♡ when West opens 1♠
♡ A Q J 7 3	♡ K 8 6 5	and East passes. If one cover
◇ A 4	◇ 8 7 5 2	card is enough for game, it is not
♣ 6	♣ 9 8 5 3	sound to open with a 1-bid.

This hand from a recent national championship illustrates the folly of super-strong 1-openings :

WEST	EAST	At one table, West opened 1 ◇
♠ A K 9 3	♠ Q J 7 4	and this was passed out! The
♡ A K 4	♡ 9 8	other table reached an ambitious
◇ A K 10 9 7	◇ 3 2	6♠ which was makeable as spades
♣ 2	♣ J 7 6 5 4	were 3-2, diamonds 3-3 and

hearts 4-4. This hand is discussed again in Chapter 10. Certainly 4♠ is an excellent contract on the actual cards, but you cannot blame East for passing 1 ◇. Give East no more than

$$\spadesuit \ Q\ J\ 10\ 7\ 4 \qquad \heartsuit \ 9\ 8 \qquad \diamondsuit \ 3\ 2 \qquad \clubsuit \ 8\ 7\ 6\ 4$$

and 6♠ *is* a good contract, while the 1 ◇ opener still languishes right there.

(3) Opener's Jump-Shift

In standard methods, this shows 19 or more points and is forcing to game. The **LTC** count should be 4-5 losers. Where 19 or more high card points are held, it is acceptable to have 5 losers, but with fewer than 19 points, a jump-shift is in order only if you have fewer than 5 losers. It would be unsound to make a droppable bid on a 4-4½ loser hand. As mentioned previously, modern systems tend to remove the 4-loser hand from a droppable 1-opening and the jump-shift then can be taken to show 19 points or more with 5 losers or any strength with 4½ losers.

Specific systems will stipulate the requirements for a jump-shift and the loser count may need to be adjusted accordingly. For example, the jump-shift in Precision, where the opening is limited to a maximum of 15 high card points, is taken to show a 14-15 hand with 5-5 shape. The loser expectancy for Precision auctions like 1♡ : 1♠, 3♣ is 5 losers. Other systems have done away with the need for a strong jump-shift entirely. Some systems play *pre-emptive* jump-shifts (0-5 points, perhaps, or 6-9 points), while others use a *constructive* jump-shift (around the 10-12 mark).

In standard methods, each of these hands is worth an opening bid of 1♡ followed by a jump-shift to 3♣ over a 1♠ or 1NT response :

♠ J 3	♠ K Q	♠ K 8	♠ 7
♡ A J 8 6 4	♡ A K 10 9 2	♡ A K 10 9 2	♡ A Q 10 9 6 2
♢ K Q	♢ 6 4	♢ 6	♢ 4
♣ A K Q J	♣ A Q J 10	♣ A Q J 10 2	♣ A K J 10 3

Opposite a jump-shift, responder should head for a slam with a fit for one of opener's suits and 8 losers or better, or 3 cover cards or better.

WEST	EAST	WEST	EAST
♠ 7 2	♠ A 8 6 4 3	♠ 7 2	♠ A 8 6 4 3
♡ A K Q 6 2	♡ 7 3	♡ A K Q 6 2	♡ 7 3
♢ A J 10 8 3	♢ K Q 9 4	♢ A J 10 8 3	♢ K Q 9 4
♣ A	♣ 4 2	♣ A	♣ K 2

WEST	EAST	WEST	EAST
1♡	1♠	1♡	1♠
3♢	4♢	3♢	4♢
4♡ (1)	4♠ (1)	4♡	4♠
4NT (2)	5♠ (3)	4NT	5♠
5NT (4)	6♣ (5)	5NT	6♢
6♢ (6)	Pass	7♢	Pass

(1) Cue bid

(2) Asking for key cards

(3) 2 key cards + trump queen

(4) Asking for kings

(5) No kings other than ♢ K

(6) A spade loser is likely

This auction is identical to the one on the left except that the reply to 5NT reveals one king. West realises that whether it is the ♠ K or the ♣ K, it will take care of the spade loser.

(4) Strong Opening Bids

(a) The Game Force

In almost every system, there is at least one action or sequence of forcing bids that commits the partnership to game. In standard methods it might be an opening bid of 2♠/2♡/2♢/2♣ each of which is forcing to game, or it might be that it is only the 2♣ (or 2♢) opening that is the game force. In standard Precision, such giant hands are shown by a 1♣ opening (forcing) followed by a jump rebid over the 1♢ negative response (e.g. 1♣ : 1♢, 2♠).

The game force opening will normally be a hand containing 22 high card points or more, but if it is only 22-23 HCP, the shape will not be balanced. A game force is warranted when the hand has less than 22 HCP if it has losers or better. All of these hands justify a force to game :

Hand A	*Hand B*	*Hand C*	*Hand D*
♠ A K Q J	♠ A K Q J 8	♠ A K Q J 8	♠ A K Q J 8
♡ A K 7	♡ A K Q 4	♡ A K Q 4 2	♡ A K 9 8 7 6
◇ A K 8	◇ 7 3	◇ 7 3	◇ 3
♣ A 5 4	♣ A 2	♣ 2	♣ 2

Hand A : Has 4 losers but with 28 HCP, a game force is essential
Hand B : Qualifies both on points and on losers.
Hand C : Only 19 HCP, but with only 3 losers, the game force is justified.
Hand D : Only 17 HCP but with 3 losers it is too risky to open with 1 ♡.

A positive reply to a game force is usually based on $1\frac{1}{2}$ quick tricks (ace and a king) or better. This is normally equivalent to two cover cards or better and thus a slam is highly likely if a trump fit comes to light. Opener figures to have a 3-loser hand and responder can cover two losers.

(b) Acol Twos

In this system, the 2♠/2♡/2◇ openings show about 8-9 playing tricks, in other words 4-5 losers. These openings are forcing for one round. The negative response is 2NT, while any positive response (again based on $1\frac{1}{2}$ quick tricks or better) commits the partnership to game. With a fit for opener, responder can explore for slam with 8 losers or 3 cover cards, and can be confident of slam potential with 7 losers or better, or 4 cover cards or better.

Acol players open 2♣, essentially a game force, on hands which have 23 HCP or more or hands of 10 playing tricks (3 losers) or better.

(c) Benjamin Twos

This is a system of 2-openings which combines twos in the majors (2♠ or 2♡ openings on 6-10 points — see next chapter) with Acol Twos in all suits (covered by the 2♣ opening) and one opening for hands worth a game force (covered by the 2◇ opening). This method is superior to standard Acol Twos because it allows opener to describe an 8-9 loser hand with a long club suit and it provides far greater definition in describing the playing strength of one-suited hands after the 2♣ opening.

Hands with 8 playing tricks or less (5 or more losers) are opened with a one-bid. Since partner needs to be able to cover at least two losers to make game opposite a 5-loser hand, partner will have to have the normal values for a response to a 1-opening (6 points or more). If partner does pass the 1-opening, there is little chance that a good game has been missed opposite a 5-loser hand.

The Benjamin 2♣ opening is best played as showing $8\frac{1}{2}$-$9\frac{1}{2}$ playing tricks ($4\frac{1}{2}$-$3\frac{1}{2}$ losers). Opener's rebid limits a one-suiter hand precisely :

2♣ : 2◇

2♡/2♠ . . . $8\frac{1}{2}$ playing tricks. Not forcing but responder bids on with one cover card or better, or even with just potential for one trick.

2♣ : 2◇

3♡/3♠ . . . 9 playing tricks (4 losers). Not forcing but responder passes only with no prospect for a trick at all. With even just potential for a cover card, e.g. a king outside, responder would bid game in opener's suit.

2♣ : 2◇

4♡/4♠ . . . $9\frac{1}{2}$ playing tricks. Game figures to be a 50% chance at worst. With 10 playing tricks (3 losers) or better, prefer to use the 2◇ game-force opening. This is because the 2♣ opener's rebid is not forcing and the 2◇ opening will give responder a better appreciation of slam potential. How would you handle the following hand :

♠ A K J   ♡ K Q J 10 7 5 2   ◇ 9   ♣ A Q

Best is to open 2♣ and rebid 4♡ over a 2◇ negative reply. Over a positive response, head for a slam. Game could fail but with 9 winners and potential for the tenth trick on a spade or club lead, the chances for success are far too good to risk being dropped below game. Where one useful queen from partner, here the queen of spades, is enough to make a game, do not make a bid below game that could be dropped.

Examples of the use of the Benjamin 2♣ opening

♠ A 3	♠ 8 7 2	♠ A	♠ K 8 7 5 2
♡ A K J 10 6 5	♡ 4 3	♡ A K J 10 6 5	♡ Q 3
◇ A K 2	◇ 6 5 4 3	◇ A K 2	◇ 8 7 5
♣ 4 3	♣ J 8 7 6	♣ 8 4 3	♣ 9 6 5

WEST	EAST
2♣ (1)	2♦
2♡	Pass (2)

(1) 4½ losers
(2) Anything above 2♡ is in jeopardy

♠ A 3		♠ 8 7 6 2	
♡ A K Q J 4 3 2		♡ 6 5	
♦ A 2		♦ 8 7 4 3	
♣ 4 3		♣ 8 7 6	

WEST	EAST
2♣	2♦
3♡ (1)	Pass (2)

(1) Shows 4 losers
(2) No prospect for a trick

♠ A 3		♠ 2	
♡ A K Q J 4 3 2		♡ 6 5	
♦ A 2		♦ 8 7 6 5 4	
♣ 4 3		♣ J 9 6 5 2	

WEST	EAST
2♣	2♦
3♡	4♡ (1)
Pass	

(1) East is not sure of a trick but the potential justifies bidding 4♡. If West held the ♠ A bare or ♠ A-K doubleton or ♠ K-Q-J, so that East has no ruffing value in spades, 4♡ would fail

WEST	EAST
2♣	2♦
2♡	2♠
3♡	4♡ (1)
Pass	

(1) East has better than 1 cover

♠ A 3		♠ K 7 6	
♡ A K Q J 4 3 2		♡ 6 5	
♦ A 2		♦ 7 4 3	
♣ 4 3		♣ 8 7 6 5 2	

WEST	EAST
2♣	2♦
3♡	4♡ (1)
Pass	

(1) The ♠ K is sufficient potential

♠ A 3 2		♠ —	
♡ A K Q J 4 3 2		♡ 8 6 5	
♦ A		♦ 8 7 6 5 4	
♣ 4 3		♣ A 9 6 5 2	

WEST	EAST
2♣	2♦
3♡	4♠ (1)
4NT (2)	5♦ (3)
6♡	Pass

(1) Splinter, showing support for hearts + spade singleton or void
(2) With less than two spade ruffs, West would sign off in 5♡
(3) One key card

The Benjamin 2♣ also works well for long minor-suit hands. Players using Benjamin Twos can play the 2NT opening to show a balanced 21-22, while the 2♦ opening followed by a 2NT rebid over a 2♡ negative can be used for balanced hands of 23-24 points. With this structure and if the partnership does not need the sequence 2♣ : 2♦,

2NT for other purposes, opener can show solid minor suit hands as follows :

2♣ : 2◇, 2NT = 8 tricks for no-trumps including a solid minor.

2♣ : 2◇, 3NT = 9 tricks for no-trumps, including a solid minor.

2♣ : 2◇, 3♣/3◇ suggests that either the minor suit is not solid or that the hand pattern does not appeal for a no-trump contract.

(5) Opener's Huge Freaks

Hands of 11 or more playing tricks are very rare, but with so few losers, slam is possible opposite next to nothing. When a game-force opener pushes to the 5-level despite no encouragement from partner, opener can be expected to hold no more than 2 losers. With 3 losers and nothing promised by partner, opener would have subsided in game. For example :

♠ A K Q J 8	♠ 4 3	♠ A K Q J 8	♠ 4 3
♡ A K Q 6 2	♡ 9 8 5 4	♡ A K Q 6 2	♡ 9 8 5 4
◇ A	◇ 7 6 5	◇ A	◇ 7 6 5
♣ Q 3	♣ J 8 7 6	♣ Q 3	♣ K 8 7 6

WEST	EAST	WEST	EAST
2◇ (1)	2♡ (2)	2◇ (1)	2♡ (2)
2♠	2NT	2♠	2NT
3♡	4♡ (3)	3♡	4♡ (3)
5◇ (4)	5♡	5◇ (4)	6♡ (5)
Pass		Pass	

(1) Benjamin game force	(1), (2), (3) & (4) as at left
(2) Artificial negative response	(5) The king of clubs, control of
(3) Support but no ace to cue	the unbid suit, must be what
(4) Cue bid, denying ace of clubs	partner is after

Where a game-force opener bids to the 6-level opposite a partner who has not promised any values, there will not be two quick losers. Opener can be expected to have 12 winners in hand or at least 11 sure winners and no worse than a 50% chance for the twelfth trick. Responder will choose the preferred 12-trick contract (if opener has bid two suits) but should bid a grand slam with a winner (ace, king or queen) in one of the suits bid by opener. However, only a cover card in opener's suit(s) will do. Winners in outside suits will almost certainly be useless ("duplication").

OPENER	Responder A	Responder B	Responder C
♠ A K	♠ 6 4 3 2	♠ 6 4 3 2	♠ 6 4 3 2
♡ A Q J 10 8 7 6 5	♡ —	♡ 4 3	♡ K 3
◇ A K Q	◇ 8 7 6 4 2	◇ 8 7 2	◇ 8 7 2
♣ —	♣ 9 8 6 4	♣ A J 7 4	♣ 9 8 6 4

Opener would start with a force to game and rebid 6♡ over responder's negative reply (e.g. 2♣ : 2◇, 6♡ . . .). Responders A and B pass 6♡ but Responder C, with a sure cover card in the king of hearts, raises to the laydown 7♡. The ♡K is worth more here than the ♣ A-K-Q-J.

OPENER	Responder A	Responder B	Responder C
♠ A K Q J 10 2	♠ 6 5	♠ 6 5 4	♠ 6 5
♡ K Q J 10 6 5	♡ 8 4 3	♡ 8 4	♡ A 4 3
◇ A	◇ 7 6 4 2	◇ 7 6 4 2	◇ 7 6 4 2
♣ —	♣ 8 7 3 2	♣ A 7 3 2	♣ 8 7 3 2

Opener starts with a force to game, rebids in spades over a negative reply and continues with 6♡ on the next round (e.g. 2♣ : 2◇, 2♠ : 2NT, 6♡). After this start, Responder A passes (prefers hearts to spades), Responder B bids 6♠ (preference for spades) and Responder C raises to 7♡ as a certain cover card, the ♡A, is held. Note that Responder C's ♡A is enough to justify bidding the grand slam while Responder B's ♣A is wasted. It does not add anything to the partnership's trick-taking capacity. Not all aces are equal.

With 13 tricks in hand or highly likely, opener can jump to a grand slam. Responder will pass or give a preference if opener has bid two suits. This hand arose in the final of a major teams event. How would you cope?

♠ A K Q J 6 3   ♡ A K Q J 6 2   ◇ A   ♣ —

At one table, the player holding these cards opened 7♠. How he must have hated it when partner put down this dummy :

♠ 2   ♡ 10 9 5 4   ◇ 7 4   ♣ K Q 7 6 5 3

Yes, spades did break 5-1 and the 7♠ opener received his just deserts when 7♠ failed while 7♡ was easy. A better approach would go like this : 2♣ (game-force) : 2◇ (negative), 2♠ : 3♣, 7♡ : Pass. Had responder preferred spades, responder would have been able to bid 7♠ over 7♡.

(6) Opener's Lesser Freaks

Hands which contain ten or more cards in two suits can be termed freak hands. These are the 5-5, 6-4, 6-5 and more extreme shapes. When partner reveals one of these shapes and you have support for one of the suits partner has shown, be enthusiastic about holding the ace, king or queen in either of partner's suits, but in the outside suits, be impressed only with aces or ace-king combinations. Holding K-Q in an outside suit may cover a loser, but there is a good chance it is opposite a singleton, so that the K-Q will not cover that loser. Holdings worse than K-Q are almost always duplicated, and thus wasted.

Suppose you knew that partner had a 6-5 pattern in hearts and clubs. If your values included A-K of spades and A-K of diamonds, the two kings would probably be wasted. They are duplication, since partner has only two cards outside the long suits and you have four high cards to cover just two losers. Two of your high cards are not needed. One king in one of partner's suits would be more valuable than the two kings outside.

Where partner has opened the bidding and has revealed a 5-5 or 6-5 or similar pattern, you would expect partner to have less than 7 losers, even for a hand with minimum opening points. The reason is that the freak shape has already eliminated two or three losers (from the normal 7 losers for a minimum opening) by virtue of the excess cards in the long suits. For example :

Hand 1	Hand 2	Hand 3	Hand 4
♠ 7 6	♠ A 6	♠ A 6	♠ 6
♡ 8 5 4 3 2	♡ 8 5 4 3 2	♡ K Q 5 4 3	♡ K Q 8 5 4 3
◇ 9 7 5 4 3	◇ K 7 5 4 3	◇ K 7 5 4 3	◇ A K 7 5 4
♣ 6	♣ 6	♣ 6	♣ 6
9 losers	7 losers	5 losers	4 losers

Hand 1 demonstrates that a 5-5 yarborough has only 9 losers (and a 6-5 yarborough would have only 8 losers).

Hand 2 has only 7 losers but you would not dream of opening with a 1♡ bid. You hold only 7 points and that is not strong enough to open with a 1-bid. Points determine the opening – losers become relevant when a trump fit has become known. However, since a 7-point 5-5 has only 7 losers, it is easy to appreciate that an opening hand with 5-5 shape is significantly better.

Hand 3 is a normal, minimum opening with a 5-5. It has a mere 12 HCP, but the loser count is only 5. The hand will be valuable if a trump fit exists. Expect a 5-5 with minimum opening points to have 5-6 losers, not 7-8.

Hand 4 is a 6-5 shape with only 12 HCP points, yet there are only 4 losers, a hand with fantastic potential if a trump fit is found but a hand that will labour badly if no trump fit exists. Expect a 6-5 pattern with minimum opening points to have 4-5 losers, not 7-8.

Because of the excellent playing potential of 5-5 and 6-5 patterns and the likelihood that partner will be able to support one of the suits if short in the other, some partnerships have specific opening bids to describe 5-5 and 6-5 shapes with less than normal opening values, say around the 6-10 HCP mark. If your system can do without a 2NT opening and does not need 2♠ and 2♡ to describe the weak twos, you can harness these openings for the weak, freak 2-suiters.

If partner has opened with a normal 1-bid and it later transpires that partner has a 5-5 or 6-5, if responder can support one of those suits, responder should calculate the partnership potential by counting opener's losers and using the cover cards in hand instead of working on responder's losers. For example :

WEST	EAST	WEST	EAST
♠ K Q 7 6 3	♠ 9 2	1♠	2♣
♡ A 9 8 4 3	♡ K 7 6	2♡	2NT/3◇ (1)
◇ K 2	◇ A 8 3	3♡	4♡
♣ 2	♣ A Q 7 4 3		
5 losers	7 losers		

(1) Use 2NT if it is forcing; if not, prefer the 3◇ fourth-suit-forcing

Working on the **LTC**, it appears that these hands have slam potential (5 + 7 = 12; 24 − 12 = 12 tricks). It is such superficial analysis that has given the **LTC** a bad name from time to time in some quarters. The reason that slam is hopeless (and even game could be a struggle if there are bad breaks in the majors) is that there is duplication in the club suit. The ♣ Q is not a working value. A superior approach for East, after West's 3♡ rebid, would be along these lines : "Partner has shown a minimum 5-5. I can expect West to have 5-6 losers. How many cover cards do I have? The ♡ K and the two aces make 3 cover cards, but I cannot count the ♣ Q as a cover card opposite a major suit 5-5. Deducting 3 cover cards from partner's 5-6 losers leaves 2-3 losers, enough for game but not for slam."

WEST	EAST	WEST	EAST
♠ K Q 9 4 3	♠ A 5 2	1◇	1♡
♡ 8	♡ K J 10 7 4	1♠	2NT (1)
◇ A Q J 6 4 2	◇ 7 3	3♠	4♠
♣ 3	♣ A J 6		
		(1) If 2NT is not forcing, use	
4 losers	8 losers	2♣ as fourth-suit forcing (over which West would bid 2♠)	

Again the loser count could give a false impression of slam potential. After West rebids the spades, East knows about the 6-5 and should place West with 4-5 losers for a minimum 6-5 opening. East can count on only 2 cover cards (the K-J-10 in hearts cannot count as a cover when West figures to be singleton or void in hearts) and thus settles for game only. Note that if East had the ♡ A instead of the ♡ K-J, East would have the same points but would have 3 cover cards and should then explore slam. In that situation, 6♠ would in fact be an excellent slam.

WEST	EAST	WEST	EAST
♠ A K 7 5 4	♠ 8 6 3	1♡	2♣
♡ A 8 6 5 3 2	♡ 7	2♠	2NT/3◇ (1)
◇ 6	◇ A 7 5	3♠	4♠
♣ 5	♣ A K J 8 7 4	Pass	
5 losers	7 losers	(1) Use 3◇ if 2NT is not forcing	

East's reasoning here would be similar to the previous situations. West's 3 ♠ confirmed a 6-5 shape. East can count on only 2 cover cards, the two aces outside partner's suits, the K-J in clubs being duplication. With just 2 cover cards opposite the expected 4-5 for a minimum 6-5 opening, East should not do more than bid the game.

WEST	EAST	WEST	EAST
♠ Q 10 7 6 5	♠ A K	1◇	1♡
♡ 3	♡ A 9 8 7 4	1♠	2NT (or 2♣)
◇ A Q J 9 4 3	◇ K 7 5	3♠	4◇ (1)
♣ A	♣ K 6 4	4NT (2)	5♣ (3)
		5♠ (4)	6◇ (5)
4 losers	6 losers	7◇ (6)	Pass

(1) East can count 4 cover cards (♠ A-K, ♡ A and ◇ K – the ♣ K is duplication). Giving opener 4-5 losers for a minimum 6-5, East can see that there is very strong slam potential. 4◇ agrees on diamonds and invites a slam. Supporting a minor suit to the 4-level is normally played as game-forcing and slam-suggesting

(2) West uses 4NT, Roman Key-Card Blackwood

(3) 5♣ shows 0 or 3 key cards, clearly 3 in view of the slam suggestion

(4) Having located all the key cards, West can tell that there is only one more critical card, the king of spades. 5♠ is an asking bid in spades

(5) East shows the king of spades by bidding 6◇ (Step 3). 5NT (Step 1) would have shown no secondary control in spades, 6♣ (Step 2) would have shown the queen, and 6♡ (Step 4) would have shown both the king and the queen. When an asking bid is made above 5-of-the-agreed-suit, it is assumed that the asker knows the key-card position, the aces, and the ask is for the king or queen of the outside suit

(6) When you have a good trump fit *and* you can tell there are no losers in the first three rounds of any suit, a grand slam is a good bet. West has located the ♠ A-K, the ♡ A and the ◇ K which tells West that there are no losers in the first three rounds of any suit. Thus 7◇ should be all right.

Quiz

1. How many losers does opener indicate with –

a. A reverse   b. A jump-shift   c. A 2♣ game-force   d. Jump-rebid of suit opened   e. 5-5 pattern and a minimum opening   f. 6-5 pattern and a minimum opening

2. Partner has revealed a hand with 5 spades and 5 hearts. Grade these 13-point hands from the most valuable for hearts to the least valuable :

A. ♠ 7   B. ♠ 7   C. ♠ 7   D. ♠ 7
    ♡ 8 7 2   ♡ 8 7 2   ♡ K Q 8   ♡ K J 2
    ◇ A K J 6 4   ◇ A K 8 6 4   ◇ A 8 6 4 2   ◇ K Q J 6 4
    ♣ K Q 7 3   ♣ A Q 7 3   ♣ A 8 7 3   ♣ Q J 7 3

Answers

1. a. 5 losers or better   b. 4   c. 3 or better   d. 5-6   e. 5-6   f. 4-5

2. Hand C is the most valuable with 4 cover cards for a heart contract. None of the high cards is wasted. Next comes Hand B which has 3 cover cards, eliminating all of opener's minor losers, but the ♣ Q is wasted. Hand A is third, with only 2 cover cards. Either the ◇ K or the club values will be wasted. Hand D is the worst with only the ♡ K sure as a cover card. If opener has one diamond and two clubs, none of responder's minor cards cover any of opener's losers.

7

Weak Twos & Other Pre-Empts

(1) The Weak Two

If used in a disciplined manner, the weak two lends itself to accurate assessment by the LTC. The requirements for a disciplined weak two (in first or second seat) are –

- About 6-10 high card points
- A good 6-card suit, headed by the Q-10 or better
- Not four cards in the other major
- No void and not two singletons

Within that framework, a normal weak two will have 7 losers (maximum) or 8 losers (minimum). For example :

♠ Q J 10 8 5 3	♠ 9 2	♠ K Q 10 9 4 2	♠ 9 2
♡ 7	♡ K Q J 8 5 3	♡ 7	♡ A K Q 8 7 6
◇ A 4 2	◇ J 10 3	◇ A 4 3	◇ 4 3
♣ 6 5 3	♣ 7 4	♣ 6 4 2	♣ 6 4 2
8 losers	8 losers	7 losers	7 losers
Minimum 2♠	Minimum 2♡	Maximum 2♠	Maximum 2♡

If the hand contains a void or two singletons, the playing strength will rise sharply and gives the weak two bid too wide a range :

♠ K Q 10 9 6 4	This hand contains 5 losers and is much too good for a weak two. It also may play better in diamonds. Ideally, your system would provide an opening bid showing a weak two-suiter, but if not, either pass or open 4♠ rather than 2♠.
♡ 7	
◇ Q J 9 8 2	
♣ 7	

♠ —	This hand has 6 losers and is too good for a weak two. Opposite A-x-x in hearts and K-x in clubs, game is a good bet. Rather than a weak 2♡, open 1♡ or 3♡ or, at favourable vulnerability, 4♡.
♡ K Q 10 7 5 3	
◇ 6 4 2	
♣ A 9 8 3	

1-Opening v. 2-Opening

With a good 6-card major and 10-12 high card points, it is not impossible to open with a 1-bid, despite the subminimum high card content. When should you choose a 1-opening and when should you prefer a weak two?

10-12 points and 6 losers : Always prefer to open with a 1-opening
10 points and 7 losers : Open with a weak two
11-12 points and 7 losers : Open with a 1-opening
10-12 points and 8 losers : Open with a weak two

♠ A 10 9 8 4 2	♠ 8 6	♠ A 9 8 5 4 2	♠ K Q
♡ 3	♡ A J 8 6 4 3	♡ J 7	♡ Q J 10 8 6 4
◇ K Q J 5	◇ K Q J	◇ K Q	◇ J 5 3
♣ 5 2	♣ 5 2	♣ J 5 4	♣ Q J
10 HCP, 6 losers	11 HCP, 7 losers	11 HCP, 8 losers	12 HCP, 8 losers
Open 1♠	Open 1♡	Open 2♠	Open 2♡

To appreciate the relative strength of these hands, give partner K-x of trumps, the A-K of clubs and another ace and gauge the chances of making game opposite each of the above holdings. Opposite the 8-loser hands, game is a poor prospect despite the point count.

Responding to the Weak Two

With 3-card or better support, use the LTC.

With 3-card support, there is a 9-card fit and the **LTC** is a better guide than point count. Since the weak two should contain 7-8 losers, responder's strategy is easy to calculate :

With 8 losers or worse : Pass (8 + 7 = 15; 24 – 15 = 9).

With 7 losers : Invite game. Bid game over a maximum reply (7 + 7 = 14; 24 – 14 = 10), but sign off in 3-Major opposite a minimum rebid by opener (7 + 8 = 15; 24 – 15 = 9).

With 6 losers : Bid game (6 + 8 = 14; 24 – 14 = 10).

With 5 losers : Explore slam. Bid slam opposite a maximum (5 + 7 = 12; 24 – 12 = 12) as long as two key cards are not missing. Settle for game opposite a minimum (5 + 8 = 13; 24 – 13 = 11).

With 4 losers or better : Insist on a slam unless you discover that two key cards are missing. You will be able to count the tricks for grand slam potential if no key cards are missing.

What action should each of the following responders take?

OPENER	Responder A	Responder B	Responder C
♠ K Q 10 7 5 2	♠ A 8 6	♠ A 8 6	♠ A 8 6
♡ A 4	♡ 7 5	♡ 5	♡ 7
◊ 9 3	◊ A K 8 5	◊ A K 8 5 4	◊ K 8 5 4
♣ 4 3 2	♣ 8 7 6 5	♣ 8 7 6 5	♣ A Q 9 6 5

Maximum 2♠

Responder A has 8 losers and should pass 2♠.

Responder B has 7 losers and should invite game. Upon learning that opener has a maximum, Responder B would bid 4♠. Had opener shown a minimum, Responder B would have signed off in 3♠. Replace opener's ace of hearts with the queen and nine tricks will be the limit.

Responder C has 6 losers and should bid 4♠. Game is highly likely, although not certain, opposite opener's maximum and should be a fair chance opposite a minimum.

Where responder has tolerance for opener – doubleton support

Since opener's range is 7-8 losers, opener will have a 5-6 playing tricks. Where responder has only doubleton support for opener and little or no prospect for ruffing any of opener's losers, it is better to calculate game and slam prospects by cover cards than by losers. Therefore :

With less than 3½ cover cards : Pass. Game worse than 50%

With 3½-4 cover cards : Invite game

With 4½-5½ cover cards : Bid game. Should be 50% or better

With 6 or more cover cards : Investigate slam potential

Responder has no fit for opener – single or void in opener's suit

Do not use the **LTC**. Normally you should pass a weak two on a misfit unless you hold 16 high card points or better (since opener's maximum is expected to be 10) and you need the full high card quota to make game when the hands do not fit.

Responder wishes to investigate game or slam potential

Your game and slam exploration opposite a weak two will be regulated by your systemic agreements. Among the best exploration conventions is the Ogust 2NT response. After 2♠/2♡ : 2NT, opener describes the strength of the hand and the number of top cards in the long suit :

3♣ = Minimum hand, one top honour

3♢ = Minimum hand, two top honours

3♡ = Maximum hand, one top honour

3♠ = Maximum hand, two top honours

3NT = Maximum hand, suit headed by A-K-Q

The top honours for answering are the A, K and Q only. Do not count the jack for the above replies. The memory guide for this convention is *Minors are minimum, 1-2-1-2-3*, where the numbers refer to the top honours held for each of the five possible replies. Where opener is between minimum and maximum, treat 8 HCP and 7 losers as maximum and 8 HCP and 8 losers as minimum. On the odd occasion, opener may use a weak two with a 7-card suit when the hand does not warrant a 3-opening. For example, when vulnerable, it would be sensible to open 2♠ with –

♠ K Q J 10 5 3 2   ♡ J 3   ♢ 8 2   ♣ 9 5

This hand does not have the 7-trick potential (6 losers) for a vulnerable 3-opening. Treat a weak two with a 7-card suit as a maximum.

Examples of the use of the Ogust 2NT response:

WEST	EAST	WEST	EAST
♠ A Q 8 7 5 2	♠ K 6 3	♠ A Q 8 7 5 2	♠ K 6 3
♡ 7 6	♡ A K 4 2	♡ 7 6	♡ A K 4 2
♢ J 8	♢ 6 5	♢ K 8	♢ 6 5
♣ 6 4 3	♣ A 8 7 2	♣ 6 4 3	♣ A 8 7 2

WEST	EAST		WEST	EAST
2♠	2NT		2♠	2NT
3♢ (1)	3♠ (2)		3♠ (1)	4♠ (2)
Pass			Pass	

(1) Minimum, 2 top honours
(2) 4 cover cards opposite 8 losers
leaves 4 losers. 9 winners

(1) Maximum, 2 top honours
(2) 4 cover cards opposite 7 losers
leaves 3 losers. 10 winners

WEST	EAST
♠ 8 3	♠ Q 7
♡ K Q 9 7 4 3	♡ A J 5
◇ 9 2	◇ A K Q J
♣ Q 4 3	♣ A K 6 2

WEST	EAST
2♡	2NT
3◇	4♡
Pass	

WEST	EAST
♠ A 3	♠ Q 7
♡ K Q 9 7 4 3	♡ A J 5
◇ 9 2	◇ A K Q J
♣ 9 4 3	♣ A K 6 2

WEST	EAST
2♡	2NT
3♠	4♣ (1)
4♠ (1)	7NT
Pass	

(1) Cue bid showing the ace

OPENER	Responder A	Responder B	Responder C
♠ A K 8 6 5 2	♠ Q J 3	♠ Q J 3	♠ Q J 3
♡ 8 3	♡ A 7 4	♡ A 7 4 2	♡ A 7 4
◇ 5 2	◇ A 9 6 3	◇ K Q J	◇ A K Q J 3
♣ 9 5 4	♣ A 8 7	♣ A 8 7	♣ K 8

Opener would start with 2♠ and each responder would use 2NT and opener would reply 3◇ showing a minimum 2♠ with two top honours, known by each responder to be the ace and king. As opener is minimum, responder can tell opener has A-K-x-x-x-x in spades and nothing more of significance. Responder A can tell that there are not ten tricks and should avoid 4♠. However, there are nine top winners and no danger suit, so that Responder A should continue with 3NT. Responder B has four tricks outside the six spade winners, but as the lead will need to be lost to set up the diamond winners, Responder B bids 4♠ and avoids 3NT. To try for no-trumps opposite a weak two, you need either instant winners or double stoppers in the outside suits. Responder C can count 12 tricks at least but chooses 6NT to protect the club holding. If the opponents do not take the ace of clubs at once, 13 tricks might be made.

(2) Other Pre-Empts

Normal pre-empts contain about 6-10 points and a good 7-card suit. Under favourable circumstances, it is feasible to pre-empt with a strong 6-card suit or with less than 6 HCP. The playing trick potential is more important than rigid adherence to the guidelines. For a 4-level pre-empt, an 8-card suit is common and less than a 7-card suit is very rare. For a 5♣ or 5♢ opening, an 8-card or 9-card suit is usual.

Pre-empts are generally based on playing strength according to the vulnerability, using the Rule of 3 and 2 (opener should hold 3 tricks less than the bid when not vulnerable, 2 tricks less when vulnerable). The situation thus lends itself to the **LTC** :

3-level pre-empt	Not vulnerable	:	7 losers
	Vulnerable	:	6 losers
4-level pre-empt	Not vulnerable	:	6 losers
	Vulnerable	:	5 losers
5♣ or 5♢ pre-empt	Not vulnerable	:	5 losers
	Vulnerable	:	4 losers

Responder can assess the combined playing strength by calculating how many of opener's losers are covered by responder's high cards. One should expect little from the pre-emptive opener outside the trump suit itself and responder should calculate the trick-taking potential as follows :

Tricks from the trump suit :

Count the ace, king and queen of trumps as 1 trick each
With trump support and a singleton : count one trick
With trump support and a void : count two tricks

Tricks outside the trump suit :

Suits headed by –

A-K-Q	=	3
A-K	=	2
A-Q	=	$1\frac{1}{2}$
A or K-Q	=	1
K-high	=	$\frac{1}{2}$
Q-high	=	0

For slam purposes, the pre-emptor might hold two key cards and the queen of trumps, but do not expect anything significantly better. Thus, if partner opens 3♠ vulnerable and you hold something like :

♠ Q 7   ♡ K Q 7 3   ◇ K 8 5   ♣ A K Q J

you have enough cover cards for 12 tricks, but you are likely to have at least two losers. Give partner A-K-J-10-x-x-x in spades and partner will not hold an ace in addition. A disciplined pre-emptor would not open 3♠ with so strong a hand. By contrast –

♠ A K J 9 5 3 2	♠ 8 7 6	♠ A K Q 8 7 5 3	♠ J
♡ 8 2	♡ 7	♡ 7	♡ A 8 4 2
◇ 7	◇ A K 8 3 2	◇ 8 6 3 2	◇ A K Q
♣ 6 5 2	♣ A K Q 4	♣ 6	♣ A K 5 4 3

WEST	EAST	WEST	EAST
3♠	4♣ (1)	4♠	4NT (1)
4♠ (2)	6♠	5♠ (2)	7♠ (3)
Pass		Pass	

(1) Used as a key card ask after a pre-empt other than 3♣. With 6 winners, slam is possible
(2) 2 key cards, no trump queen

(1) Key card ask. With 6 winners, slam is highly likely
(2) 2 key cards + trump queen
(3) 7NT if you need a top badly

Quiz

1. How many losers should opener have for these actions?

a. Weak two opening, maximum
b. 4◇ opening, vulnerable
c. 3♠ opening, not vulnerable
d. 5♣ opening, not vulnerable

2. You opened 2♡, weak. What is your reply to partner's 2NT Ogust?

A. ♠ 4 3	B. ♠ Q 3	C. ♠ 4	D. ♠ 4
♡ K Q 10 8 6 5	♡ K Q 10 8 6 5	♡ K Q 10 8 6 5	♡ A Q 10 8 6 5
◇ 6 2	◇ 6 2	◇ K 6 2	◇ J 6 2
♣ A 7 4	♣ 10 7 4	♣ 8 7 2	♣ J 8 2

3. ♠ 4
    ♡ K 8 6 4
    ◇ A K Q J
    ♣ A 8 4 3

Partner opened 3♡ with neither side vulnerable. What action should you take : Pass? Bid game? Explore slam? If you head for a slam and ask for aces, what is your rebid for every reply opener could make?

Answers

1. a. 7 losers   b. 5 losers   c. 7 losers   d. 5 losers

2. A. 3♠ – maximum, 2 top honours   B. 3◇ – minimum, 2 honours
c. 3♠ – 8 HCP + 7 losers = maximum   D. 3◇ – 8 losers = minimum.

3. With 5 losers opposite 7, you have slam potential and should ask for aces. If partner has no ace, stop in game. Opposite one ace, bid 6♡ but if partner turns up with two aces, bid 7NT. There are 13 winners opposite –

♠ A 5   ♡ A J 10 7 5 3 2   ◇ 6 4   ♣ 7 2

8

No-Trump Bids and the LTC

The **LTC** is not used to assess no-trump contracts but knowledge of the number of cover cards contained by a balanced hand is useful when responder has a long suit, particularly a 7-card or longer suit, since given that partner has a balanced hand, a sound trump suit is known to exist. A guide to the number of cover cards expected is as follows :

Points expected	Cover cards expected	Losers needed for major suit game	Losers needed for a small slam
0-6	1 if lucky	4	2
7-9	2	5	3
10-12	3	6	4
13-15	4	7	5
16-18	5	8	6
19-21	6	9	7
22-24	7	10	8
25-27	8	11	9

Bidding Major Suit Games

(a) Responder has a 7-card or 8-card suit

Deduct the cover cards expected from partner's range from your losers. If the answer is 3 (or 2), bid the major suit game. If the answer is 4 or more, be satisfied with a partscore or, with a borderline decision, invite game.

♠ 8 7	♠ A J 6 5 4 3 2	♠ A 8 6 2	♠ 5
♡ K Q 4	♡ 8 6 2	♡ 10 5	♡ J 9 8 7 6 4 3 2
◇ A K 7 4	◇ 5	◇ A K 9 3	◇ 8 5
♣ A 9 6 3	♣ 7 2	♣ K Q 6	♣ 7 4

WEST	EAST		WEST	EAST
1NT	4♠ (1)		1NT	4♡ (1)
Pass			Pass	

(1) 8 losers. 5 cover cards expected. Game is about an 80% chance

(1) 8 losers. 5 covers expected. 4♡ depends on a 2-1 trump break

The weaker the responding hand in high cards, the more responder will have to depend on opener having a fair share of aces. Give the West on the right hand pair of hands K-Q-J-2 in spades rather than A-8-6-2 and game will probably fail (unless declarer can sneak a spade trick). However, the above examples illustrate the potential when responder has a very long suit and it would be anti-percentage to settle for a partscore. Note that opener has the worst possible support for responder's suit. Give opener three trumps in each case and the chance of game rises.

(b) Responder has a 5-card or 6-card suit

Here the trump suit may be inadequate. There is a huge difference between A-J-x-x-x-x-x opposite x-x or A-J-x-x-x-x opposite x-x-x (chance of one loser about 60% in each case) and A-J-x-x-x-x-x opposite x-x (chance of one loser less than 20%. Where responder has a 6-card suit, responder will need to determine that opener has 3-card support or better before applying the cover cards and losers from the above tables. If that cannot be conveniently determined, then add one loser to your tally before applying the tables. In other words, opposite a 16-18 1NT, responder with a 6-card major should bid game in the major with 7 losers and only invite game with 8 losers if unable to confirm that opener holds three cards or more in the major. Likewise, with a 5-card suit, responder needs to establish that opener has 4-card support in order to use the cover cards and loser tables on page 79.

RESPONDER	Opener A	Opener B	Opener C
♠ A 9 7 6 4 3	♠ 8 5	♠ 8 5	♠ 8 5 2
♡ 8	♡ A K 3 2	♡ A K Q 2	♡ A K 3
◇ K 8 5	◇ A 9 2	◇ A 9 2	◇ A 9 2
♣ 7 5 2	♣ K Q 6 4	♣ K Q 6 4	♣ K Q 6 4

After a 15-18 or 16-18 1NT opening, responder should transfer to spades and then raise to 3♠ (1NT : 2♡, 2♠, 3♠ . . .). This shows a *six*-card suit and invitational values. Opener A would pass, as the spade holding is minimum and the cover cards held are no more than expected. The chance of making 4♠ opposite Opener A is about 34% (needs spades to be 3-2 *and* the club finesse). Opener B would accept the invitation and bid 4♠. While the spade holding is minimum, there is one cover card more than expected. The chance of making 4♠ opposite Opener B is a bit below 68% (spades 3-2 is enough, as long as there is no club ruff). Opener C should accept the invitation and bid 4♠ even though the hand is minimum in high card content and flattish in shape. If the 3-card support for the known 6-card suit is appreciated, then game prospects will be upgraded. Opener should realise that responder would have bid 4♠ direct if responder had held a 7-card suit. The chance of making 4♠ opposite Opener C is about 66% (either a 2-2 spade break or the ♣A onside).

Bidding Minor Suit Games

(a) You hold a 7-card or 8-card suit

Deduct the cover cards expected in partner's range from your losers. If the answer is 2, bid the minor suit game. If the answer is 3 or more, be satisfied with a partscore or consider a contract of 3NT.

WEST	EAST	WEST	EAST
♠ A 7 5 2	♠ 3	♠ A 8 6	♠ —
♡ A K 4 2	♡ 8 6	♡ A K 5	♡ 7 2
◇ K Q 4	◇ 9 8 6	◇ K Q 9 3	◇ 8 5 2
♣ 9 6	♣ K Q J 7 5 4 2	♣ 10 9 6	♣ K J 8 7 5 4 3 2

WEST	EAST	WEST	EAST
1NT	5♣ (1)	1NT	5♣ (1)
Pass		Pass	

(1) 7 losers. 5 covers expected. Game is about a 50% chance, depending on the diamond position. 3NT is highly likely to fail

(1) 7 losers. 5 covers expected. Game is about 75%, failing only if both the ace and the queen of trumps are offside

Where responder's long suit is headed by the ace, 3NT stands a much better chance, since the ace itself provides a ready entry. Without the ace, a weak hand with a very long minor is best played in the minor.

(b) You hold a 5-card or 6-card minor

Without exceptional length, such hands are usually just as good, and sometimes much better, in 3NT. With the values for game, prefer 3NT unless you can diagnose that opener has inadequate cover opposite a short suit. Some modern systems are able to reveal a short suit with responder and allow the 1NT opener to choose between 3NT and responder's minor. Opener naturally bases the decision on whether the short suit is adequately stopped. The more strength there is opposite the short suit, the more attractive 3NT becomes and the more duplication there is for a trump contract.

Bidding Slams

(a) You hold a 7-card or 8-card suit

Deduct the cover cards expected from partner's range from your losers. If the answer is 1 (or 0) investigate slam prospects. In addition to having adequate trick-taking potential, you must be able to ensure that there are not two key cards missing for a small slam or one key card missing for a grand slam. Suppose that partner has opened 2NT (around 22-23 points) and you hold :

♠ K J 9 8 6 5 4 2   ♡ 7 6   ◇ 8   ♣ 4 3

The trump suit is excellent and you have 7 losers. Partner's cover card expectancy in the 22-24 zone is around 7, so that you have potential for a grand slam and are highly likely to make a small slam, despite your low high card count. Initially, transfer to spades by bidding 3♡ and over opener's 3♠, bid 4NT, asking for key cards. What would you reach opposite each of the following hands?

Opener A	*Opener B*	*Opener C*	*Opener D*	*Opener E*
♠ A 3	♠ A 3	♠ A 3	♠ A 3	♠ A 3
♡ K 9 8	♡ K J 8	♡ A 9 8	♡ A K 8	♡ A K Q J
◇ A K Q 4	◇ A K J 4	◇ A K J 4	◇ A K 9 4	◇ A 9 5 2
♣ K Q J 2	♠ A Q 8 2	♣ A Q 8 2	♣ A 8 7 2	♣ A 7 6

Opener A will reply 5♡ and responder will know two key cards are missing so that the auction will end in 5♠. Opener B shows 3 key cards and so responder will bid 6♠. Played by opener, 6♠ is excellent since, if there is no trump loser (about a 90% chance), any lead but a trump will give you a contract and even on a trump lead, chances for success are very high.

Openers C, D and E all reveal that there are no key cards missing. Responder can now count on 11 tricks (8 spades and 3 aces) and tries for a grand slam by 5NT, asking for kings and promising all key cards are held. Opener C shows one king and responder settles for a small slam. Opener D shows two kings and that is enough for responder to bid 7NT. Opener E has only one king but when responder bids 5NT, the reply should be 7♠, not 6◇, because of the certain extra winners from the heart suit. What more could responder want? Responder should convert this to 7NT. What would surprise many players is that a grand slam is not only feasible but is biddable with such low point count.

Similarly, a 7-loser hand with a 7-card suit should explore a slam :

RESPONDER	Opener A	Opener B	Opener C
♠ 8 4	♠ K 9 5	♠ A 9 5	♠ A 9 5
♡ A Q 9 8 6 5 2	♡ K 7 4	♡ K J 3	♡ K 7 3
◇ 9	◇ A K 2	◇ A J 7	◇ A 2
♣ 8 6 3	♣ A K Q 10	♣ A K Q 2	♣ A K Q J 2

After the 2NT opening, responder would bid 3◇ as a transfer to 3♡ and continue with 4NT, a key card ask. Opener A's reply would show that one key card was missing and responder would settle for 6♡. The answer from Opener B accounts for all the key cards, but the reply to 5NT does not enable responder to bid the grand slam. With Opener C, there are also no key cards missing, but when responder bids 5NT, opener should bid the grand slam because of the tricks produced by the club suit.

(b) You hold a 6-card or a 5-card suit

First, determine the soundness of the trump suit. If a trump fit exists, deduct partner's expected cover cards from your losers. If the answer is 1 or 0, check on the key cards before committing your side to a slam :

OPENER	Responder A	Responder B	Responder C
♠ A Q J 8 7 6	♠ K 5 4	♠ 9 5 4	♠ K 5 4
♡ 6	♡ Q J 3	♡ K Q J	♡ A 9 5
◇ K 8	◇ A 7 5 3	◇ A Q J	◇ A 7 5 3
♣ K Q J 2	♣ A 7 4	♣ 10 7 5 3	♣ A 7 4

In a standard approach, the bidding might commence 1♠ : 2NT, showing 13-15 balanced, 3♣ by opener and 3♠ preference by responder. With only 4 losers and 4 cover cards expected from the 13-15 partner, opener enquires with 4NT. Responder A replies 5♣ showing 0 or 3 key cards. As it cannot be zero, opener bids 6♠ as one key card is missing. Responder B bids 5◇, showing 1 or 4 key cards. As it could be just one key card, opener must sign off in 5♠ which is itself in some jeopardy. Responder C also bids 5◇ to show 1 or 4 key cards but when opener attempts to sign off in 5♠, responder must bid on if 4 key cards are held. How many more could partner possibly need? When bidding on in this kind of situation, bid Step 1 to deny the queen of trumps and Step 2 to show the queen of trumps. On the actual hand, Responder C would bid 5NT to deny the trump queen. When opener realises that responder has four key cards, not one, opener will bid 7NT.

♠ K Q J 6 5	♠ A 7 3	♠ K Q J 6 5	♠ A 7 3
♡ A Q J 6 2	♡ K 5	♡ A Q J 6 2	♡ K 5
◇ 2	◇ A 10 6 3	◇ 4 2	◇ A J 6 3
♣ A 4	♣ K 9 5 2	♣ A	♣ Q J 7 4

WEST	EAST	WEST	EAST
1♠	2NT	1♠	2NT
3♡	3♠	3♡	3♠
4♣ (1)	4◇ (1)	4♣ (1)	4◇ (1)
4♡ (1)	5♣ (2)	4♡ (1)	5♡ (2)
5◇ (2)	5♡ (2)	6♠ (3)	Pass
5NT (3)	6◇ (4)		
7♠ (5)	Pass		

(1) Cue bid, first round control
(2) Cue bid, second round control
(3) Trump ask
(4) One top trump honour
(5) West has located the four vital cover cards to bid the grand slam. At pairs, the risk of 7NT is justified

(1) Cue bid, first round control
(2) Cue bid, showing the king of hearts and denying both minor suit kings (bypassing 5♣ and 5◇)
(3) West now knows that one vital cover card, a minor suit king, is missing. Consequently, a grand slam is too risky. At pairs, 6NT is the best choice

♠ K Q J 6 5	♠ A 7		♠ K Q J 6 5	♠ 8 7
♡ A Q J 6 2	♡ K 5 4 3		♡ A Q J 6 2	♡ K 5 4 3
◇ 4 2	◇ A 9 8		◇ 4 2	◇ A K 8
♣ A	♣ K 8 6 3		♣ A	♣ K J 4 2

WEST	EAST		WEST	EAST
1♠	2NT		1♠	2NT
3♡	4◇ (1)		3♡	4◇ (1)
4NT (2)	5♣ (3)		4NT (2)	5♡ (3)
5NT (4)	6◇ (5)		6♡ (4)	Pass
7♡ (6)	Pass			

(1) Cue bid, heart support and the ◇ A, denying the ♣ A
(2) Key card ask
(3) 0 or 3 key cards
(4) Any outside kings?
(5) One king outside trumps
(6) At pairs, 7NT is reasonable

(1) Cue bid, heart support, showing the ◇ A and denying the ♣ A
(2) Key card ask
(3) 2 key cards, no trump queen
(4) With one key card missing, the grand slam will be a bad bet. 6NT is a poor choice, depending essentially on the spade position

9

Overcalls, Takeout Doubles and Sacrifice Bidding

(A) Overcalls

The 1-Level Overcall

The expectancy for a disciplined overcall at the 1-level is a strong 5-card suit, 8-15 HCP and 8 losers (minimum) up to 6 losers (maximum). A 9-loser hand is generally too weak and a 5-loser hand is too strong. The following are suitable for a 1♠ overcall :

♠ K Q J 7 2	♠ A K Q 8 6	♠ A Q 8 7 3	♠ A 10 9 6 2	♠ K Q J 5 2
♡ 8 5 3	♡ 5 3 2	♡ 9	♡ 5	♡ 4 3
◇ 8 2	◇ 9 7	◇ K 8 3	◇ A K 8 2	◇ 8 6 3
♣ K 9 6	♣ 7 4 2	♣ 9 8 5 4	♣ K 9 5	♣ A K Q
8 losers	8 losers	7 losers	6 losers	6 losers

The following are not suitable for a 1♠ overcall :

♠ A 7 6 4 2	♠ K Q J 5 4	♠ A Q J 7 3 2	♠ A Q J 8 7 6 4
♡ J 3	♡ 8 4	♡ A 8	♡ 2
◇ K 7 6	◇ 7 6 4	◇ A	◇ A 7 4
♣ J 5 4	♣ J 7 2	♣ 7 6 4 3	♣ 5 4
9 losers, too weak	9 losers, too weak	5 losers, too strong	6 losers, but use a pre-empt bid

Responding to the 1-Level Overcall

As partner should hold a good 5-card suit, 3-card support will do. With support and potential ruffing values, use the **LTC**, adding your losers to partner's minimum of 8 and then bidding for the appropriate number of tricks. With support and no ruffing values, estimate your cover cards and deduct from partner's minimum losers (8) to determine how high you should raise. Partner can calculate your losers (by adding your bid – in tricks – to 8 and deducting the answer from 24) or your cover cards (by deducting your bid – in tricks – from 13 and deducting that from 8). If partner has better than 8 losers and a higher contract is thus warranted, partner can then bid on.

The partner of the overcaller is called the "advancer" and raises by the advancer contain the values described below. Suppose the bidding has been :

WEST	NORTH	EAST	SOUTH
1♣	1♠	Pass	?

The available raises for South (the advancer) are :

2♠ = 8 losers (8 + 8 = 16, 24, 24 – 16 = 8 playing tricks)
    or 3 cover cards (8 — 3 = 5 losers = 8 playing tricks)

3♠ = 7 losers *or* 4 cover cards

4♠ = 6 losers *or* 5 cover cards

6♠ = 4 losers *or* 7 cover cards

In the above auction, what action should South take with these hands?

Advancer A	*Advancer B*	*Advancer C*	*Advancer D*
♠ 8 7 6	♠ A 7 6	♠ J 7 6 5 4	♠ K Q 7 2
♡ J 6	♡ 7 6	♡ Q 3	♡ J 8
◇ K Q 5 4 3	◇ K Q 5 4 3	◇ J 8 7	◇ A 9
♣ 9 8 2	♣ 9 8 2	♣ 8 4 2	♣ 7 6 4 3 2

Advancer E	*Advancer F*	*Advancer G*	*Advancer H*
♠ A 8 7 2	♠ A 8 7 2	♠ K 9 7 6 2	♠ A 9 7 6 4 2
♡ 9 4	♡ 9 4	♡ A K 7 4 3	♡ A K 7 4 3 2
◇ 7 6 4 2	◇ A 7 6 4	◇ 6 4	◇ —
♣ K Q 2	♣ K Q 2	♣ 5	♣ 7

Advancer A: Pass. You have 9 losers and your support is poor. To bid here may well urge partner to bid too much. Pass first and if they compete further, support to 2 ♠ *on the next round*. That will not sound encouraging.

Advancer B: Bid 2♠. You have 8 losers. 8 + 8 = 16; 24 – 16 = 8 tricks.

Advancer C: Pass. Despite your support, your hand is terrible (11 losers). The hand does not warrant a pre-emptive raise because of its balanced shape. If you must take action, try some psychic bid.

Advancer D: Bid 3♠. You have 7 losers (8 + 7 = 15; 24 – 15 = 9 tricks).
Advancer E: Bid 2♠. You have 8 losers and good support.
Advancer F: Bid 3♠. You have 7 losers and good support.
Advancer G: Bid 4♠. You have 6 losers and excellent support.
Advancer H: Bid 6♠. You have only 4 losers and magnificent support.
The real concern is whether you are missing 7♠. If your system is able
to discover that partner has the ♠K and the ♣A and not three hearts,
then you are well-placed to judge whether 7♠ is a good contract.

Where the advancer holds a strong supporting hand but is unsure
how high to raise, standard technique is to use a cue bid of the enemy
suit. This sort of hand contains extra high card values but too many
losers to warrant bidding game. Some partnerships use a structure
known as "cue-raises" to distinguish raises based primarily on
strength from raises based primarily on shape. Suppose the bidding
has been :

WEST	NORTH	EAST	SOUTH
1◇	1♠	Pass	?

Using cue-raises, South's immediate supporting actions are as
follows :

8 losers	2♠ = raise on shape, weak in high cards, pre-emptive	2◇ = worth a raise to *two*, strong, flattish, 3 cover cards
7 losers	3♠ = raise on shape, weak in high cards, pre-emptive	3◇ = worth a raise to *three*, strong, flattish, 4 cover cards
6 losers	4♠ = raise on shape, weak in high cards, pre-emptive	4◇ = worth a raise to *four*, strong, flattish, 5 cover cards

If the opponents compete further, direct raises (weak in defence)
encourage partner to sacrifice; cue-raises (strong in high cards)
encourage partner to defend. Where advancer's hand seems too good
for just game or the final destination is not certain, it is best initially to
bid the enemy suit at the cheapest level and then bid again. Slam-going
hands with support for partner (very rare after just an overcall) may
make a cue-raise at the 4-level and then bid again. These types of action
tend to occur when playing against opponents who are prone to
psyching.

2-Level Overcall in a Minor e.g. (1♡) : 2♣ *or* (1♡) : 2◇ *

A simple overcall in a minor suit at the 2-level (not a jump) shows a strong 5-card or 6-card suit, 10-15 HCP and an expectancy of 7 losers (minimum) to 6 losers (maximum). On the odd occasion, a very strong 6-card suit may be overcalled with a loser count of 8. A 5-loser hand would be too strong. These hands would be suitable for a 2♣ overcall :

♠ A 7	♠ J 6	♠ 6 4	♠ 7 5
♡ 8 4 2	♡ J 8	♡ Q 2	♡ 4 2
◇ 7 3	◇ 8 4 3	◇ 7 3 2	◇ A K 4 2
♣ A Q 9 8 6 4	♣ A K J 10 6 4	♣ A K Q 9 8 5	♣ A Q J 10 3
7 losers	8 losers	7 losers	6 losers

With support, advancer raises, based on losers or on cover cards :

Raise to 3-level = 8 losers *or* 3 cover cards

Raise to 4-level = 7 losers *or* 4 cover cards

Raise to 5-level = 6 losers *or* 5 cover cards

Pass = More than 8 losers or less than 3 cover cards

On most good hands, advancer's objective will be 3NT rather than 5-minor and accordingly, advancer will often prefer not to raise but to bid 2NT, 3NT, or cue bid the enemy suit to preserve no-trump chances. With a hand suitable for no-trumps, advancer should choose as follows :

3 cover cards only : Raise minor to the 3-level. If partner can envisage 3NT opposite just 3 cover cards, partner can bid 3NT (with a stopper in their suit) or bid their suit (to ask you for a stopper).

4 cover cards : Bid 2NT with their suit stopped and generally around 12-14 HCP. With no stopper, bid the enemy suit.

5 cover cards : Bid 3NT with their suit stopped and generally around 15-17 HCP. With no stopper, bid the enemy suit.

---

*In describing bidding, a useful convention is to place bids by the opponents in parentheses and bids by your partnership without parentheses. Thus, 1♡ : 2◇ refers to bids made only by your side (with the opponents passing) while (1♡) : 2◇ means that an *opponent* opened with 1♡ and 2◇ was bid by your side.

In this area, 3NT will be feasible with significantly less than 26 points where the minor suit is running and the outside winners are immediate (instant winners, such as aces, A-K or A-K-Q combinations which do not entail losing the lead). Advancer should upgrade the hand when holding a top honour in partner's suit and aces in the outside suits, as well as having their suit stopped. When the hand contains kings rather than aces and no high card in partner's minor, a double stopper or better is needed in the enemy suit. The overcaller should upgrade the hand when holding aces outside the long suit or when the long suit is solid (A-K-Q-x-x-x) or missing just the king (A-Q-J-x-x-x) since the king figures to be with right-hand opponent if partner does not have it.

The (1♠) : 2♡ Overcall

Play the 2♡ overcaller to hold a strong 5-card or longer suit, 10-15 HCP and 7 losers (minimum) to 6 losers (maximum). 5 losers is too good.

Raise to 3♡ = 8 losers *or* cover cards. Partner bids 4♡ if maximum.

Raise to 4♡ = 7 losers *or* 4 cover cards.

With stronger hands, worth a slam try, advancer should cue bid the enemy suit first, raise the hearts next. With clearcut slam values (very rare after the opposition opened the bidding), bid 4NT as a key card ask.

Overcalls After a Pre-Empt

A suit bid at the 3-level should show an excellent suit and better than a minimum opening hand. A good guide for a 3-level overcall, such as (3◇) : 3♠, is a 6-loser hand in the direct seat and a 6-7 loser hand in the pass-out seat. An overcall at the 4-level, such as (3♠) : 4♡ or (3◇) : 4♡, should be a 5-loser hand in the direct seat or in the pass-out seat. With a 4-loser hand after a 3-level pre-empt, the best approach is to double first and bid game in your suit next. For example :

WEST	NORTH	EAST	SOUTH
3◇	Double	Pass	3♠
Pass	4♡ . . .		

North should hold an excellent heart suit and a 3-4 loser hand.

When partner overcalls at the 3-level and advancer has support :

0-2 cover cards : Pass
3 cover cards : Raise to the 4-level
4 cover cards : Raise a minor to the 5-level, a major to game
5 cover cards or more : Explore slam prospects

♠ K 9 8 3	♠ 7 6	♠ K 9 8 3 2	♠ 7 6
♡ K 4 3	♡ A Q J 7 6 2	♡ K 4 3	♡ A Q J 7 6 2
◇ A 7 5	◇ K Q J	◇ 8 7 5	◇ K Q J
♣ 8 5 3	♣ Q 4	♣ 8 5	♣ Q 4
3 cover cards	6 losers	2 cover cards	6 losers
WEST	EAST	WEST	EAST
(3♣)	3♡	(3♣)	3♡
4♡	Pass	Pass	

The preceding examples also demonstrate how the concept of cover cards complement the concepts in the **LTC**. Note that both West hands have 9 losers, yet game is an excellent chance on the first set (on the reasonable assumption that the ace of spades is onside) while 4♡ is hopeless on the second set. Where partner is known to have a good long suit, and you have support but no ruffing value, cover cards work better than losers.

Jump Overcalls

e.g. (1◇) : 2♠   *or*   (1♡) : 3♣   *or*   (1♠) : 3♡ . . .

There are four popular treatments of the single jump overcall :

Weak Jump Overcalls (WJOs) : About 6-10 HCP, 6 card or longer suit and 8 losers (minimum) to 7 losers (maximum). WJOs are used primarily for pre-emptive purposes.

Intermediate Jump Overcalls (IJOs) : About 11-15 HCP, 6-card suit at least, 7 losers (minimum) to 6 losers (maximum). A 5-loser hand would be too strong. The IJO is equivalent to an opener repeating the suit opened at minimum level e.g. (1◇) : 2♠ = 1♠ : 1NT, 2♠ or (1♡) : 3♣ = 1♣ : 1◇, 2♣. IJOs have a combination of constructive and pre-emptive functions.

Strong Jump Overcalls (SJOs) : About 16-19 HCP, a good 5-card or longer suit, a one-suited hand containing 6 losers (minimum) to 5 losers (maximum). A hand of just 4 losers would be too strong. With a 2-suited or 3-suited hand in the 16-19 HCP range, double first rather than use the strong jump overcall. SJOs are essentially constructive.

Roman Jump Overcalls (RJOs) : These are 2-suiters where the jump-overcall shows the suit bid and the next suit along (excluding the suit bid by the opposition). For example, (1 ◇) : 2♡ shows hearts *and* spades, while 2♠ would show spades *and* clubs, and 3♣ would show clubs *and* hearts. The suits should be at least 5-carders and with good texture. The high card content need not be great (8-13 HCP is normal) but the **LTC** should be around 6-7 losers. With more losers, the hand is too weak and with fewer losers, take a stronger action. With 5 losers, double first and bid one of the suits next; with 4 losers or better, a jump to 2NT is used.

Over the jump to 2NT, advancer is obliged to bid the cheapest suit (other than theirs) and then the overcaller bids 3NT (showing the two unbid suits) or bids a suit (showing the suit bid *and* the suit which advancer was forced to bid). For example :

WEST	NORTH	EAST	SOUTH
1 ◇	2NT	Pass	3♣
Pass	?		(forced)

If North now bid 3NT, that would show spades and hearts (advancer is naturally forced to take this out and choose the preferred major *or*, with no preference, bid 4 ◇ to ask partner to choose the major). If, instead, North bid 3♡, that would show hearts and clubs *and four losers*, while 4♡ would show hearts and clubs *and 3 losers*.

Which variety of jump overcall should be used?

Clearly it is an important matter for partnership agreement whether WJO, IJOs, SJOs or RJOs should be used. If the partnership has no clear preference, the following recommendations will be helpful :

Weak Jump Overcalls : Best used at duplicate pairs, particularly by a strong pair against weak opposition. Not as effective against competent opponents.

Intermediate Jump Overcalls : Best used for teams events or at duplicate pairs against strong opposition.

Strong Jump Overcalls : Best reserved for novice partnerships or when playing casual rubber bridge.

Roman Jump Overcalls : Very effective when they arise. Best used only by a strong partnership. Work well against strong opposition.

After the Weak Jump Overcall (7-8 losers)

(a) After a jump to 2-major, e.g. (1♦) : 2♠ . . .

The situation is comparable with a weak two opening and if third player passes, advancer should continue as though partner had opened with a weak two (see Chapter 7, page 86). If third player bids and you can support partner's suit, raising partner to the 3-level would show 7 losers (or 4 cover cards) and raising partner to game would require 6 losers (or 5 cover cards). Where the third player raises opener's suit, some partnerships use a double by advancer as a takeout double which would include an invitational raise of the overcalled suit. For example, after :

WEST	NORTH	EAST	SOUTH
1♦	2♠	3♦	?

3♠ = 8 losers or 3 cover cards. Purely competitive. Not a game invitation.

4♠ = 6 losers or 5 cover cards.

Double = For takeout, including an invitational raise (7 losers/4 cover cards). With a minimum jump overcall, partner simply repeats the suit overcalled (3♠) or may make any cheaper bid (over which advancer will give preference back to the overcalled suit). Obviously, the partnership must have cleared the meaning of this double in advance. If double is used for penalties, then advancer cannot incorporate competitive, invitational *and* game-going hands in the space available.

(b) After a weak jump to 3-minor, e.g. (1♡) : 3♣ . . .

With a flattish hand, prefer to try for no-trumps than the minor game. Bid 3NT with their suit stopped and around 4-5 cover cards, or bid their suit to ask partner for a stopper. If supporting, with a genuine prospect for game :

Raise to 4-level = 6 losers or 5 cover cards

Raise to 5-level = 5 losers or 6 cover cards

After the Intermediate Jump Overcall (6-7 losers)

(a) After a jump to 2-major, e.g. (1♢) : 2♠ . . .

If third player passes, the situation can be treated in exactly the same way as after a weak two opening, except that partner's range is 11-15 HCP, not 6-10 HCP, and correspondingly, advancer needs less strength to take equivalent actions. If you regard the IJO as a minimum opening hand with a 6-card suit, the principles are easy to grasp. If advancer has support :

9 losers : Pass or raise to the 3-level (pre-emptive)

8 losers/3 cover cards : Invite game (via the 2NT Ogust Convention)

7 losers/4 cover cards : Bid game.

If third player bids, supporting partner to the 3-level replaces the 2NT invitation. For example :

WEST	NORTH	EAST	SOUTH
1♢	2♠	3♣	3♠ (1)

(1) 8 losers or 3 cover cards, inviting game. A 4♠ bid is one trick better.

Alternatively, some partnerships prefer to use the 3-level raise as purely competitive, the raise to game as normal (6 losers/5 cover cards) and a competitive double which includes raises with invitational values (see the preceding section on bidding after a weak jump overcall).

(b) After an intermediate jump to 3-minor, e.g. (1♡) : 3♣ . . .

With a flattish hand, prefer no-trumps. Bid 3NT if you have their suit adequately covered and around 3-4 cover cards, or bid their suit to ask partner for a stopper :

WEST	EAST	WEST	EAST
♠ A 8 3	♠ 6 2	♠ 7 6	♠ A 8 2
♡ A 7 6	♡ 4 3	♡ A K 4	♡ J
◇ 7 6 4 2	◇ A Q J	◇ J 9 8 7	◇ Q 4 3
♣ A 9 8	♣ K Q J 7 6 4	♣ A 9 8 2	♣ K Q J 7 6 4

WEST	EAST	WEST	EAST
(1♠)	3♣	(1♠)	3♣
3NT	Pass	3♠	3NT
		Pass	

In each of the above cases, it is far superior to land in 3NT (which is unbeatable) than to pursue the minor suit game. If advancer is not interested in no-trumps, but intends to support the overcalled suit with genuine game prospects :

Raise to 4-level = 7 losers / 4 cover cards

Raise to 5-level = 6 losers / 5 cover cards

After the Strong Jump Overcall (5-6 losers)

(a)   After a jump to 2-major, e.g. (1◇) : 2♠ . . .

If advancer has support :

10 losers or worse : Pass

9 losers : Raise to the 3-level

8 losers : Raise to game

Slam prospects : Cue bid their suit

(b) After a strong jump to 3-minor, e.g. (1♡) : 3♣ . . .

With a flattish hand, prefer no-trumps. Bid 3NT if you have their suit adequately stopped and 2-3 cover cards, or bid their suit to ask partner for a stopper. If supporting partner's minor :

Raise to the 4-level = 8 losers / 3 cover cards

Raise to the 5-level = 7 losers / 4 cover cards

After the Roman Jump Overcall (5-6 losers)

The Roman Jump Overcall is different from the other jump overcalls, since it shows a 2-suiter, not a 1-suiter. While the hand need not be strong in high cards, the loser count is low since the hand is at least a 5-5 shape. Even a 5-5 yarborough has only 9 losers, so that with A-x-x-x-x and K-Q-x-x-x, the loser count would drop to 6. The suits shown are the suit bid and the next suit up, so that (1♦) : 2♡, say, shows hearts and spades, while 2♠ would show spades / clubs, and 3♣ would show clubs/hearts.

Whenever possible, advancer will select one of the suits shown and a bid of 3NT would be strong with the outside suits well-covered. When advancer intends to support, advancer may pass the suit bid, give preference to the other suit or raise either suit. Advancer should gauge the hand strength by using cover cards, counting the A, K or Q in either of partner's suits as full cover cards and only the ace in an outside suit as a full cover card.

(a) After a Roman Jump to the 2-level, e.g. (1♣) : 2♦

With 0 or 1 cover card, pass or give preference to the second suit. With support for a major, raise to the 3-level with 2 cover cards and bid game with 3 cover cards. With 4 cover cards, slam is possible and with 5 cover cards or more, slam is likely. You could use 2NT as an enquiry or bid the enemy suit or bid 4NT if aces is the only problem. With support for the minor, sign-off with 0-2 cover cards, invite game with 3 cover cards and insist on game and probe for slam with 4 cover cards or better.

(b) After a Roman Jump to the 3-level, e.g. (1♠) : 3♦

With 0-2 cover cards, pass or give preference at the 3-level. Bid game in a major or raise a minor to the 4-level with 3 cover cards. With 4 cover cards or more, insist on game and explore slam possibilities.

WEST	EAST	WEST	EAST
♠ J 5 3	♠ A Q 8 6 4	♠ 3	♠ A Q 8 6 4
♡ 8 7 4 2	♡ 6 5	♡ 9 8 7 4 2	♡ 6 5
♦ A Q J	♦ 8	♦ A Q J 6	♦ 8
♣ 6 4 2	♣ K 9 8 7 5	♣ 6 4 2	♣ K 9 8 7 5

WEST	EAST	WEST	EAST
(1♦)	2♠ (1)	(1♦)	2♠ (1)
Pass		3♣	Pass

(1) Showing spades and clubs

WEST	EAST	WEST	EAST
♠ K 5 3 2	♠ A Q 8 6 4	♠ K 7 5	♠ Q J 8 6 4
♡ 8 4	♡ K Q 7 6 2	♡ A 9 4 3	♡ K Q 7 6 2
◇ A 9 8	◇ 7	◇ A 8 4 2	◇ 7
♣ J 9 5 3	♣ 6 2	♣ J 5	♣ 6 2

WEST	EAST	WEST	EAST
(1♣)	2♡ (1)	(1♣)	2♡
3♠ (2)	4♠ (3)	4♡ (1)	Pass

(1) Showing hearts and spades
(2) 2 cover cards, inviting game
(3) 5 losers, maximum, accepts

(1) 3 cover cards are enough to bid a major game with a trump fit opposite a Roman Jump Overcall

Pre-Emptive Overcalls

A pre-emptive overcall skips *two* levels of bidding, e.g. (1◇) : 3♠ *or* (1♣) : 3◇ *or* (1♡) : 4♣ *or* (1♠) : 4♡ . . . Note that the sequences (1◇) : 3♣ *or* (1♡) : 3♣/3◇ *or* (1♠) : 3♣/3◇/3♡ are jump-overcalls. They may be weak bids if the partnership has so stipulated (see pages 106-107) but they are not included here as pre-emptive overcalls.

The principles for pre-emptive overcalls are the same as for pre-emptive openings. You need a very long suit and a weakish hand. Assess your playing tricks and add 3 if not vulnerable, 2 if vulnerable (Rule of 3 & 2). If the total allows you to skip two levels of bidding, make the pre-emptive overcall. If not, simply overcall at the cheapest level. For example :

♠ K Q J 8 7 6 4	If they open 1♣, bid 3♠ if you are not
♡ 7	vulnerable, but overcall just 1♠ if you are
◇ Q 9 7	vulnerable (unless you are using weak jump
♣ 4 3	overcalls, when a jump to 2♠ is reasonable when vulnerable).

Pre-emptive overcalls of 4♡ and 4♠ are treated a little differently to first-seat or second-seat pre-emptive openings of 4♡ or 4♠. The latter are normally limited to 10 HCP while 4♡ or 4♠ openings in third-seat or fourth seat and pre-emptive overcalls of 4♡ or 4♠ may hold more than 10 HCP (up to 15 HCP is acceptable) since slam is so unlikely either after partner has passed already or after the opposition have opened the bidding. These 'sound' 4♡ and 4♠ openings or overcalls are used on hands which contain about 8 playing tricks.

Bidding after a pre-emptive overcall is the same as bidding after a pre-emptive opening (see Chapter 7, pages 90-92).

Hands Too Strong for a Simple Overcall or a Jump-Overcall

Hands with a long suit and 16 HCP or more or 5-loser hands or better are too strong for a simple overcall or even a jump-overcall (unless you are using strong jump overcalls, but even then, hands of 4 losers or better are too good for a strong jump). Hands which are too strong for a simple overcall or a jump overcall are shown by doubling first and bidding the long suit on the next round :

Double and Bid New Suit Next = 5-card or longer suit, with 16 HCP or better or a 5-loser hand if less than 16 HCP. For example :

WEST	NORTH	EAST	SOUTH
1 ◇	Double	Pass	1 ♠
Pass	2 ♡ . . .		

or :

WEST	NORTH	EAST	SOUTH
1 ♠	Double	Pass	2 ♡
Pass	3 ♣ . . .		

Double and Jump New Suit = 5-card or longer suit, usually 19 HCP or better or a 4-loser hand if less than 19 points. For example :

WEST	NORTH	EAST	SOUTH
1 ◇	Double	Pass	1 ♡
Pass	2 ♠ . . .		

or :

WEST	NORTH	EAST	SOUTH
1 ◇	Double	Pass	1 ♠
Pass	3 ♣ . . .		

Double and Jump To Game = Long, strong suit, $3\frac{1}{2}$ losers :

WEST	NORTH	EAST	SOUTH
1 ♣	Double	Pass	1 ◇ or 1 ♠
Pass	4 ♡ . . .		

Double and Cue Bid Their Suit = 3-loser hand or better, forcing to game. For example :

WEST	NORTH	EAST	SOUTH
1 ◇	Double	Pass	1 ♠
Pass	2 ◇ . . .		

The same meaning (3 losers or better) would attach to an immediate cue bid of the enemy suit, if the partnership plays this as a powerhouse game-force (standard). However, many pairs prefer to use the cue bid of the enemy suit as some other convention (e.g. Michaels Cue Bids).

Suppose West opened 1 ♡. North doubled and South replied 2 ♣. What action should North take next on each of these hands :

NORTH 1	NORTH 2	NORTH 3	NORTH 4
♠ A K J 8 6	♠ A K 9 8 6 4	♠ A K Q 7 4	♠ A K J 8 7 6
♡ 7 4 3	♡ K 8	♡ A 3	♡ A K
◇ A 9 8	◇ A 9 7 4	◇ K Q J 6	◇ A Q J
♣ K Q	♣ 6	♣ 4 2	♣ 9 7

(1) Bid 2 ♠, showing five or more spades, 16 points or better.

(2) Bid 2 ♠, showing five or more spades and a 5-loser hand if less than 16 HCP.

(3) Bid 3 ♠, showing five or more spades and a 4-loser hand.

(4) Bid 4 ♠, showing a long strong spade suit and 3½ losers. 4 ♠ is not a certainty but is a good chance even opposite a yarborough (if partner has three spades). Since partner will not bid with a yarborough if you rebid just 3 ♠, you should take the gamble yourself.

(B) Takeout Doubles

At the 1-level

The takeout double at the 1-level is expected to contain 12 HCP or more. If the hand contains 12-15 HCP, it should include a shortage (doubleton or less) in the opposition's suit. If the opponents have bid two suits, the doubler should be short in at least one of those suits. With 16 HCP or more, the shortage requirement is attractive but not obligatory.

The LTC expectancy for a takeout double at the 1-level is 7 losers or better. Just as an opening hand's expectancy is 7 losers or better, but it can occasionally be found to contain 8 losers, so a takeout double may occasionally be found to have 8 losers. Where the count is below 12 HCP, the **LTC** should be 6 to compensate for the deficiency in high cards. Each of the following hands is worth a takeout double of 1♡ :

♠ A 7 5 3	♠ A Q 7 4	♠ A J 6 5	♠ Q J 7 4
♡ 9	♡ 8 4	♡ J 4	♡ —
◇ K J 7 5	◇ K Q 3	◇ K J 2	◇ K 9 8 3
♣ A 9 8 3	♣ J 9 7 4	♣ A 8 6 3	♣ A 8 6 4 2
7 losers	7 losers	8 losers	6 losers

Takeout double after passing

After passing initially, you may make a takeout double with a shortage in the opposition suit and a maximum pass, normally 10-11 HCP (12 HCP would be rare for a passed hand with a shortage). The **LTC** should be 7, but 8 losers would be acceptable if the hand contains fillers (10s and 9s). Each of these hands would be suitable for a double of 1♡ after passing :

♠ K Q 7 2	♠ Q J 6 3	♠ K Q 8 7	♠ K Q J 5
♡ 8 4	♡ 8	♡ 7	♡ 9 5
◇ A Q 6	◇ A 8 5 3	◇ A 8 5 3	◇ A 10 9
♣ 9 7 4 3	♣ K 9 7 2	♣ 8 6 4 3	♣ J 10 7 3
7 losers	7 losers	7 losers	8 losers

Responding to the 1-Level Takeout Double

Advancer must reply unless there is an intervening bid or advancer is so powerful in the opponent's suit as to make a penalty pass attractive. The standard structure of replies to a takeout double is along these lines :

0-5 points : Bid a suit at the cheapest level. Do not bid 1NT. If third player bids, pass with this weak range.

6-9 points : Bid a suit at the cheapest level or bid 1NT. Do not jump. With a choice of actions, bid a major rather than 1NT but prefer 1NT to a minor suit. If third player bids, bid your suit anyway but not more than one level higher than if third player had passed.

10-12 points : Reply as normal but with a single jump, either in a suit or in no-trumps, with the usual major/no trumps/minor order of preference. If third player bids, make a jump bid in your suit anyway (not beyond game, of course) or if you were about to jump to 2NT, you may still bid 2NT which is taken as 10-12, even over 2-level intervention (not 6-9).

13 points or more : Bid a game, if the best spot is clearcut, otherwise bid the opposition suit to create a game-forcing auction (or near game-forcing – some pairs use the bid of the enemy suit to create a forcing situation until suit agreement is reached – a sensible arrangement). The same actions can be used if third player bids over the double.

The same ranges can be dealt with in terms of the **LTC** when you wish to respond to partner's takeout double with a suit bid :

9 losers or worse : Bid your suit at the cheapest level. If third player bids, make your suit bid anyway with 9 losers, pass with 10 losers or worse.

8 losers : Make a jump response in your suit. If third player has not bid, quite a sensible agreement is that a major suit jump to the 2-level shows 8 losers and a 4-card suit and a major suit jump to the 3-level shows 8 losers and a 5-card or longer suit. For example :

WEST	NORTH	EAST	SOUTH
1♣	Double	Pass	2♡
			8 losers, 4-card suit

WEST	NORTH	EAST	SOUTH
1♣	Double	Pass	3♡
			8 losers, 5-card suit

7 losers : Here you would be worth a bid of game in a major if you could be certain that the trump fit is sound. If you have a 4-card major, you cannot be sure, since partner may have only 3-card support. There are two reasonable approaches with a 4-card major :

(1) With 9-11 HCP, make just a jump-response and expect partner to raise with 4-card support, even with only 7 losers, *or*

(2) Cue bid the enemy suit and then if partner bids your major or

supports your major, bid game. This is fine if you hold 12 HCP or more, or if a trump fit is found, but with less than 12 HCP it is dangerous since you will be committing your side to game with inadequate values if no trump fit is found.

Where you have 7 losers and a 5-card major, it is safe to jump to game in the major if partner is a disciplined doubler and can be relied on to hold tolerance (3 cards) or support (4 or more cards) in unbid majors. If this is not certain in your partner or your system, then prefer to use a cue bid of the enemy suit and bid your suit later. The drawback to undisciplined doubles and the need to rely on the cue bid of their suit is that it may be difficult to convey to partner that you have a 5-card or longer suit below 3NT . . . you often run out of bidding space before the length of your suit can be revealed.

With 6 losers or better : This would be a rare situation, but if it occurs, start with a cue bid of the enemy suit. If your values are mainly based on shape, slam will not be likely, but if the high card content is strong, especially in controls (aces and kings) than a slam is feasible if a good trump fit is located and the partnership has 12 losers or better. Quite a useful arrangement is to play that a cue bid of the opponent's suit at the 4-level agrees partner's suit as trumps and is an invitation to a slam. Thus :

WEST	NORTH	EAST	SOUTH
1♡	Double	Pass	2♡ (1)
Pass	2♠	Pass	4♡ . . . (2)

(1) Cue bid of their suit = game-force (or near game-force)
(2) Agrees spades, invites slam

If partner does not wish to accept the invitation (having a minimum double), partner can sign off in game. If accepting, partner can make a cue bid or use 4NT to ask.

Rebids by the Doubler

If advancer replies to your double with a suit bid, you need to interpret partner's reply and if a trump fit exists, act according to the combined losers. Be wary of applying the **LTC** when you hold only 3-card support.

Advancer's Action	Doubler Has Support
Advancer bid a suit at the cheapest level (third player did not intervene) : Advancer can be expected to hold a 4-card suit and 9 losers or worse.	6-7 losers or worse : Pass. Game chances are remote. 5 losers : Raise 1-level. Advancer should bid on with 2 cover cards. 4 losers : Jump-raise. Advancer should bid on with 1 cover card. 3 losers : Bid game.
Advancer bid at suit at the cheapest level over 3rd player's intervening bid : Advancer can be expected to hold a 4-card suit and a 9-loser hand.	7 losers or worse : Pass. 6 losers : Raise to 2-level, but if advancer's bid was already at the 2-level, prefer to pass. 5 losers : Jump-raise to 4-level.
Advancer jump bids a suit (with or without intervention by 3rd player) : Expect advancer to hold at least a 4-card suit and 8 losers. If it is exactly a 4-card suit, advancer may have 7 losers.	After jump to 2-level : Pass with 8 losers or 7 losers and 3-card support only. With 7 losers and 4-card support, raise to 3-level. With 6 losers, raise to 4-level. After jump to 3-level : Pass with 8 losers or 7 losers and 3-card support only. With 4-card support and 7 losers or better, bid game in a major, raise minor to 4-level.
Advancer cue bids the enemy suit : Expect advancer to hold 12 HCP or more, 7 losers or better.	After a trump fit appears, be content with game with 6-7 losers, but slam may be possible with 5 losers or better.

Example Hands

WEST	EAST	WEST	EAST
♠ 6 4	♠ A Q 8 7	♠ K Q	♠ A J 8 7
♡ Q J 4 2	♡ A K 5	♡ Q J 4 2	♡ A K 5
◇ J 7 3 2	◇ 9 6	◇ J 7 3 2	◇ 8 4
♣ 6 5 2	♣ J 8 7 4	♣ 6 5 2	♣ Q 9 8 3
10 losers	7 losers	9 losers	7½ losers

WEST	EAST	WEST	EAST
(1◇)	Double	(1◇)	Double
1♡	Pass	1♡	Pass

WEST	EAST	WEST	EAST
♠ 9 6 3 2	♠ A K 7	♠ 9 6 3 2	♠ A K 7
♡ A 9 8 2	♡ K Q J 5	♡ 10 9 8 2	♡ K Q J 5
◇ 4 3	◇ 7	◇ 4 3	◇ 9
♣ 8 5 4	♣ A K 6 3 2	♣ 8 5 4	♣ A K 6 3 2
1 cover card	4 losers	No cover card	4 losers

WEST	EAST	WEST	EAST
(1◇)	Double	(1◇)	Double
1♡	3♡	1♡	3♡
4♡	Pass	Pass	
7 losers	7 losers	8½ losers	6 losers

WEST	EAST	WEST	EAST
♠ 7 6 4 2	♠ A Q 9 8	♠ K 7 6 2	♠ A Q 9 8
♡ A 2	♡ Q J 9 7 3	♡ A 2	♡ Q J 9 7 3
◇ 7 6 5	◇ A K	◇ 7 6 5	◇ A K
♣ 9 8 4 2	♣ 7 3	♣ 9 8 4 2	♣ 7 3
1 cover card	5 losers	2 cover cards	5 losers

WEST	EAST	WEST	EAST
(1♣)	Double	(1♣)	Double
1♠	2♠ (1)	1♠	2♠
Pass (2)		4♠ (1)	Pass

(1) Double + bid again = 5 losers
(2) 1 cover card is not enough

(1) 2 cover cards opposite 5 losers
= 3 losers = 10 tricks

WEST	EAST	WEST	EAST
♠ K 9 6 4	♠ A Q 8 7	♠ K 2	♠ A J 6 5 4
♡ 6 3	♡ A 8 7 2	♡ 8 7 3 2	♡ A K 6 5
◇ Q 10 2	◇ J 9	◇ A J 8	◇ 9 2
♣ A Q 9 8	♣ K 3 2	♣ Q 7 6 5	♣ K 3

WEST	EAST	WEST	EAST
(1◇)	Double	(1◇)	Double
2♠ (1)	3♠ (2)	2♡ (1)	4♡
4♠	Pass	Pass	

(1) 7 losers but only a 4-card suit
(2) 7 losers but 4-card support

(1) Too good for just 1♡. Bid even a weak major rather than 1NT.

WEST	EAST	WEST	EAST
♠ K 8 5 3	♠ A 9 7 4	♠ Q J 10 6 4 3	♠ A 9 7 2
♡ Q 2	♡ J 6	♡ A K 7	♡ 8 2
◇ Q 9 3 2	◇ A K 5	◇ 6	◇ K 5 4
♣ A 8 6	♣ J 7 5 3	♣ 9 4 2	♣ K Q 7 3

8½ losers	8 losers	7 losers	7 losers

WEST	EAST	WEST	EAST
(1♡)	Double	(1♡)	Double
2♠	Pass	4♠ (1)	Pass

(1) Too good for just 2♠ or 3♠

Doubles at the 2-Level

A 2-level double will occur when third player raises opener's suit or bids a new suit at the 2-level or after a weak-two opening. The requirements for the double are the same as for a 1-level double, but the **LTC** of a 2-level double should not be 8 losers or worse. Even 7½ losers is doubtful and you should aim for a sound 7 losers or better, because the room for responder to judge game prospects has been severely curtailed.

The standard responses to a 2-level double are similar to the responses to a 1-level double. With 9 losers or worse, bid your suit at the cheapest level, with 8 losers jump bid a major (even if this involves bidding game, such as a jump to 4♡ after a double of 2♠), and with 7 losers, bid game in a major or jump bid a minor to the 4-level (if no trump is impractical). To bid a minor suit game, you should have a 5-loser hand.

There is far less accuracy in this approach than after a 1-level double and some strong partnerships opt for a different approach using the 2NT Lebensohl Convention. In this method, a 2NT reply to a 2-level double is artificial and requires the doubler to bid 3♣ on any ordinary double. Advancer will either pass 3♣ with a weak hand with club length or will bid another suit to show a weak hand, 9 losers or worse. In other words, advancer's 2NT is a prelude to a weak sign-off. If doubler is not prepared to be passed in 3♣ (because the hand is too good), doubler will make some other natural bid. Any suit bid by advancer at the 3-level without using the Lebensohl 2NT is encouraging, showing an 8-loser hand, while with 7 losers, advancer would bid game or cue bid their suit.

WEST	EAST	WEST	EAST
♠ J 4 2	♠ 7 6	♠ J 4 2	♠ 7
♡ K 8 5 3	♡ A 9 7 4	♡ K Q 5 4	♡ A 7 3 2
◇ 6 4	◇ A Q 9 8	◇ 4	◇ K Q 8 7 6
♣ 7 6 5 3	♣ K Q J	♣ K 5 4 3 2	♣ A J 9
10 losers	6 losers	7 losers	6 losers

WEST	EAST	WEST	EAST
(2♠)	Double	(2♠)	Double
3♡ (1)	Pass	4♡ (1)	Pass

(1) Using Lebensohl, West would bid 2NT and rebid 3♡ as a sign-off over East's puppet 3♣

(1) Too strong for a mere 3♡. Even if using Lebensohl, 4♡ is the bid

Doubles Over 3-Level Pre-Empts

The doubler should have a shortage in the opposition's suit and have support or tolerance for the missing suits. The **LTC** should be 6 or better in the direct seat and 7 or better in the pass-out seat. The advancer's best approach when bidding a suit in reply to this double is to base the action on cover cards.

If bidding a major :
2 cover cards or less : Bid the major at the cheapest level.
3-4 cover cards : Jump bid the major to game.
5 cover cards or more : aim for a slam.

If bidding a minor :
3 cover cards or less : Bid the minor at the cheapest level.
4 cover cards : Bid game.
5 cover cards or more : Aim for a slam.

Where advancer bids a suit at the cheapest level, the doubler should still bid on to game if 2 cover cards with advancer would be enough for a game. While the advancer may indeed have nothing at all, the percentage action is not to play partner for a yarborough but for about 6-8 points and if partner has that much, 2 cover cards will often be held. It is the profit of the pre-emptor to pressure you into decisions such as these.

WEST	EAST	WEST	EAST
♠ 8 6	♠ A Q J 3	♠ 8 6	♠ K J 9 7
♡ A 9 8 3	♡ K 7 6 2	♡ J 5 4 3 2	♡ A Q 9 6
◇ A 7 4	◇ J 6	◇ 7 6 5 4	◇ A J 8 3
♣ K 5 4 2	♣ A Q 3	♣ Q 5	♣ 7
3 cover cards	6 losers	No cover cards	6 losers

WEST	EAST	WEST	EAST
(3◇)	Double	(3♣)	Double
4♡	Pass	3♡	Pass

WEST	EAST	WEST	EAST
♠ 5 3 2	♠ A Q J 4	(3◇)	Double
♡ A 7 6 5 4	♡ K Q 8 3	3♡	4♡ (1)
◇ 8 2	◇ 7	Pass	
♣ Q 5 4	♣ A 9 8 3		
2 cover cards	5 losers		

(1) Could fail if West's hand is hopeless but to pass is also risky

(C) Sacrifice Bidding

A sacrifice is the deliberate acceptance of a loss in the expectation that the opposition were going to make their contract and the hope that the loss incurred by bidding higher will be less than the loss if they made their contract. It clearly makes sense to accept a loss of 100 or 300 if the opponents were about to make a game which would gain them 620. On the other hand, it is not attractive to take a loss when the opponents were not going to make their contract. Why should you be minus when you could have been plus?

The first decision to make before taking a sacrifice is whether the opponents are likely to make their contract. If your side has reasonable defensive prospects, it is foolish to sacrifice. Give the defence a chance if there is a real chance. A good working guide is that you should not "save" (= take a sacrifice) if you have a 1-in-3 chance of defeating them. This will naturally depend on the number of defensive tricks you have in your hand and what you estimate partner is likely to have. For example, if partner has an opening hand, you can reasonably expect two defensive tricks, an overcall might have one defensive trick while a pre-emptor is likely to have no defensive trick at all.

Once you have decided that they are likely to make their contract *and* you have established a strong trump fit, then the **LTC** provides an excellent guide to your prospects in your sacrifice. It will indicate the number of tricks you can expect to win and the loss you will thus incur, given that the opponents will surely double you. If this loss is less than the value of their contract, take the save. If the loss exceeds the value of their contract, pass and accept your fate.

Examples

♠ J
♡ K Q 8 7 6 4
◇ 8 7 6
♣ 8 5 2

The bidding has been (1 ♠) : Double : 4 ♠ : to you. Should you bid 5 ♡? You provide no defensive tricks and partner may have 2-3 tricks, so they will almost surely make their game. You are bound to have a good heart fit and you have 8 losers. Partner should have 7 losers so that you figure to go two down (8 + 7 = 15; 24 − 15 = 9 tricks). If they are vulnerable, their game is worth 620, so that vulnerable (− 500) or not (− 300), the save is worthwhile. If they are not vulnerable, their game is worth 420. You should bid 5 ♡ not vulnerable (− 300) but if vulnerable, the cost of two down doubled, − 500, is too great and you should pass.

♠ K 8 7 5 2
♡ 7 5
◇ 8
♣ J 9 8 4 3

Partner opened with a weak 2♠ and right-hand opponent passed. What would you do?

Clearly you cannot expect to make game, but equally clearly they are certain to make a game and possibly a slam. (Partner has at most 10 points and less than 4 hearts, so they have at least 26 points and at least 8 hearts and at least 8 diamonds. If one of them is void in spades, about a 50-50 chance, they could even make a grand slam.) You have 8 losers and the weak two should have 7-8 losers, so that you figure to make 8 or 9 tricks in spades. If you are vulnerable and they are not, your worst position, you should still bid 4♠. If you play 4♠ doubled and go one down, you will have a great result and even – 500 if you are two down may be all right if they have a slam available. At any other vulnerability, you should be even more energetic in pulling the wool over their eyes. The very least you could do would be to bid 4♠, but depending on the gullibility of the opponents, you could try a psychic 4NT Blackwood (naturally signing off in 5♠ when partner produces insufficient aces) or a psychic 2NT Ogust (a better bluff against strong opponents) or even a psychic 3♡, new suit forcing. They may have their work cut out to unravel the auction after any of these psyches and you can always run to the haven of the spade suit.

♠ 9 7 4
♡ J 8 4 3
◇ J 7 2
♣ A 9 6

Partner opened 3♣, not vulnerable versus vulnerable. Right-hand opponent bid 4♠. What should you do? Even though you have no defence against 4♠, you should not bid 5♣. Firstly, as you have only 1 cover card and partner should have 7 losers, 5♣ doubled would be four down, – 700, more than the value of their game. Further, it is highly likely that they can make a slam (maybe a grand slam). Your best chance is to pass 4♠ and hope that they do not push on to a slam. If so, partner's pre-empt has reaped a great reward, while if you bid 5♣, you may well goad them into a slam as they realise that neither of them has any wasted strength in clubs. You will find that it almost never pays to sacrifice with a flat hand.

♠ 8 4 3   Left-hand opponent opened 1♠, partner
♡ K 7 6 3   bid 2NT and right-hand opponent jumped to
◇ 6   4♠. Your move? While it is conceivable that
♣ K 9 6 5 2   you might beat 4♠ (if partner plays ace, king
                             and another diamond to give you a ruff and
your ♡K scores), this scenario is also wildly unlikely. You have 8
losers, partner for a 5-5 shape in the 8-12 point zone, figures to have 6-7
losers, so that you should make 9-10 tricks. At any vulnerability, the
sacrifice is worthwhile. If you are vulnerable and they are not,
partner's 2NT should be highly respectable and you can confidently
expect not to be more than one down (unless you know that your
partner's bidding is not to be trusted in this area).

♠ A K 4   Left-hand opponent opened 1♡, partner
♡ 8 6   bid 2♠ (weak) and right-hand opponent
◇ K Q 7 4   jumped to 4♡. What should you do? There are
♣ 9 6 5 3   vague chances of defence, but one opponent is
                             likely to be short in spades, so that you cannot
count on more than one spade trick and one diamond trick and
partner's weak jump overcall is not likely to produce more than one
defensive trick, if that. Partner should have 7-8 losers and you produce
2 certain cover cards in spades and one probable cover card in
diamonds (not sure, since partner may hold a singleton diamond).
Deducting your cover cards from partner's losers, you should be able
to make 8-9 tricks. Again, the save is worthwhile at any vulnerability,
since two down doubled will be less than their game, except at adverse
vulnerability, but then partner's weak jump overcall should be based
on 7 losers, not 8 (subject to partner's suicidal tendencies), and you
figure to be only one down, perhaps even making if partner has a
surprise fit for the diamonds, for example something like :

♠ Q J 10 9 7 5 2   ♡ 7 4   ◇ A 10 2   ♣ 8

Quiz

1. How many losers should partner have for each of these auctions?

a. Takeout double of 1 ◇
b. Intermediate jump overcall
c. Simple overcall at the 2-level
d. Takeout double and single raise of your minimum suit reply

e. Weak jump overcall
f. Raising your 1-level overcall to two
g. Minimum suit reply to your double
h. Takeout double and a jump raise of your minimum suit reply

2. The bidding has been (1♠) : 2♡ : (2♠) : to you. What action should you take in reply to partner's 2♡ overcall?

A. ♠ 8 2	B. ♠ 8 2	C. ♠ K Q 8	D. ♠ 4
♡ Q 8 7	♡ Q 7 4 2	♡ A 8 6 4	♡ A J 8 3
◇ A K 4 3 2	◇ Q J 7 4 3	◇ 7 4	◇ 6 2
♣ 6 4 3	♣ 7 6	♣ A 9 5 2	♣ A 9 8 6 5 4

3. Partner doubled the opening bid of 1♡ and third player passed. What action should you take in reply to the double on these hands?

A. ♠ J 5	B. ♠ 6 5 4 3 2	C. ♠ Q J 10 6 4 3	D. ♠ 9 7 6 5 4
♡ 5 4 3	♡ 10 8 2	♡ A K 7	♡ A J 3 2
◇ 7 6 2	◇ 7 3	◇ 6	◇ 8 6
♣ A K Q 4 3	♣ K 7 5	♣ 9 4 2	♣ 9 8

E. ♠ K 9 6 4	F. ♠ 4 3	G. ♠ A 2	H. ♠ J 6
♡ 6 3	♡ A 9 8 2	♡ 8 7 5	♡ K Q
◇ Q 3 2	◇ 9 6 3 2	◇ 7 6 4	◇ J 4 3 2
♣ A Q 9 8	♣ 8 5 4	♣ A K Q 8 5	♣ 9 8 7 5 2

4. You hold the same hands as in Question 3 and again partner has doubled 1♡, but this time third player raises to 2♡. What do you do now?

5.

	WEST	NORTH	EAST	SOUTH
	1◇	Double	Pass	1♠
	Pass	?		

What action should North take next with these hands?

A. ♠ K J 8 3	B. ♠ Q J 10 3	C. ♠ A Q 9 8	D. ♠ A K 8 7 5 3
♡ K 9 7 2	♡ A K Q	♡ Q J 9 7 3	♡ A J 10 9
◇ A 2	◇ 8	◇ 8 5	◇ 6
♣ Q J 4	♣ A Q J 8 2	♣ A K	♣ A Q

E. ♠ A 2　　F. ♠ A 6　　　G. ♠ K Q　　　H. ♠ A K 2
　♡ A K J 8 5　　♡ A K 3　　　♡ K Q J 8 7 6　　♡ A Q J 10 2
　♢ 8 5　　　♢ 8 4　　　　♢ 5　　　　　♢ —
　♣ K Q 9 8　　♣ A K Q 9 7 4　　♣ A Q 9 2　　♣ K Q 9 8 4

Answers

1. a. 7 or better　b. 6-7　c. 6-7　d. 5　e. 7-8　f. 8　g. 9 or worse　h. 4

2. A. 3♡　B. Pass. Partner will not let the bidding die in 2♠. 3♡ is too encouraging.　C. 3♠ and follow with 4♡. You are worth 4♡, but the drawback in bidding 4♡ is that if the opener bids 4♠, partner may bid 5♡ without giving you the chance to double 4♠.　D. 4♡ – 7 losers opposite 7.

3.　A. 3♣　B. 1♠　C. 4♠　D. 1♠　E. 2.♠　F. 2♢　G. 2♡
H. 2♣

4. A. 3♣　B. Pass　C. 4♠　D. 2♠　E. 3♠　F. Pass　G. 3♡
H. If using a responsive double, that is best, asking partner to pick a minor, if not, 3♣.

5. A. Pass　B. 3♠　C. 2♠　D. 4♠　E. 2♡　F. 3♣　G. 3♡
H. 2♢

10

Adjustments to The Losing Trick Count

Adjustments (1), (2) and (3) are discussed in former texts and analysed here. Adjustments (4) and (5) have not been dealt with previously.

(1) Opening the bidding

A misconception common to many of the older **LTC** guides is that opening the bidding can proceed according to the number of losers held. This example appears in *The Losing Trick Count* by Courtenay and Walshe (first published 1935) :

♠ A Q 7   ♥ K 8 5   ♦ A J 6   ♣ 8 6 3 2

"Total 8 losers, and not even an opening bid," say the authors. Yet no competent player would pass on such values today. The high card content is more than enough to open, with the hope of ending in some number of no-trumps. Imagine if you were to pass on such a hand and partner were to do the same. You would have passed in an almost certain game.

In Harrison-Gray's excellent pamphlet *The Losing Trick Count* (1961), this is the recommended approach :

"An opening bid of One is made with :

  (a) not more than 7 losers;
  (b) adequate high card values, including two defensive tricks;
  (c) a sound rebid.

Exceptions : hands with 8 losers but good controls (three quick tricks or better), balanced hands with 13 or more points that are suitable for No-trump play, and tactical third-in-hand openings."

With all these qualifications and exceptions, there is little point in having any loser requirement when judging whether to open the bidding. Jeff Rubens in his outstanding *Secrets Of Winning Bridge* (1969) takes the use of losers for opening the bidding to its absurd conclusion :

". . . in the basic **LTC**, the following is not an opening bid (8 losers) :

♠ A x x x   ♥ A x x   ♦ A x x   ♣ A x x

but the following is (7 losers) :

♠ Q x x x x x   ♥ x x x x x   ♦ x   ♣ x

The over-valuation of the second hand can be corrected easily by stipulating defensive-trick requirements for an opening bid. (It is not necessary for responder – this hand is worth a game bid if partner opens in a major suit!) However, the undervaluation of the first hand can be corrected only by a major adjustment . . ."

All of the problems can be eliminated if one does not try to invest the **LTC** with super powers, as an all-purpose, omnipotent valuation guide which does away with point count and other techniques for hand valuation. For opening the bidding, the high card content of the hand will be the relevant factor and should be stipulated by the system used. A sound standard approach is to open all hands with 13 HCP and those with 12 HCP that have no defects (such as singleton honours). The **LTC** can be used for borderline hands and your system could stipulate that hands of 11 HCP may be opened with 6 losers and hands of 10 HCP with 5 losers.

The **LTC** can be usefully employed for opening bids when the opening is based on trick-taking capacity rather than high card content. For example, for pre-emptive openings the dominant requirement is the playing strength and for that, the **LTC** is an accurate gauge. Even there, the high card content remains relevant since most systems will have an upper limit for pre-emptive openings (about 10 HCP in standard methods).

Furthermore, in opening two-bids which promise a certain number of playing tricks, the **LTC** is useful to estimate the playing tricks held. For example, if using Benjamin Twos, the **LTC** can categorise a hand as a 2 ♦ opening (game-force type, 3 losers or better) or as a 2 ♣ opening (more limited, $3\frac{1}{2}$-$4\frac{1}{2}$ losers). Here again, however, the high content will be relevant since, just as the maximum high card content for a pre-empt is stipulated, so the system will almost certainly set a minimum high card holding for such a two-opening (usually around 16 HCP or better).

Conclusion : The **LTC** should not be used as a primary guide for opening the bidding, but can be used as an adjunct for borderline hands or to judge the playing tricks when that is part of the criteria for opening. The **LTC** normally comes into play only later in the bidding after a fit in a trump suit has become established.

(2) Is the queen a winner or a loser?

According to Courtenay and Walshe : "All Queens in the hand must be balanced by Aces (not necessarily in the same suit), unless such Queens are in a sequence of honours, e.g. K-Q-J, Q-J-10 . . .

♠ A 8 5 4 2   ♡ K Q 9 7   ◇ Q 6 3   ♣ 4

In this example, there are two Queens and only one Ace. Therefore the Q-6-3 of Diamonds must be counted as 3 losers."

Simple commonsense revolts against this proposition. Whatever the value of Q-6-3 may be, it is preferable to a holding such as 7-6-3 which would also be valued as 3 losers. Q-x-x is better than nothing at all.

According to Harrison-Gray :

"Some distinction must obviously be made between A-x-x, K-x-x and Q-x-x. The first is a better two-loser holding than K-x-x, and three losers must be counted in a Queen-high suit unless :

    (a) it is the proposed trump suit;
    (b) the suit has been bid by partner;
    (c) the Queen is supported by the Knave;
    (d) the Queen is 'balanced' by the Ace in another suit.

♠ Q 9 2   ♡ 8   ◇ 10 9 5   ♣ A Q 10 8 3 2

Over 1♡ or 1◇, bid 2♣. Note : ♠Q not balanced. ♣A used to balance* ♣Q."

Jeff Rubens put it this way :

"I suggest adjusting on the basis that a king is an average high honour. If all your high cards are kings or if you have the same number of aces as queens (which balance out), keep the standard LTC. But if you have more aces than queens, subtract $\frac{1}{2}$ loser for each extra ace; similarly, if you have more queens than aces, add $\frac{1}{2}$ loser for each extra queen. Thus :

---

*The term 'balance' in these contexts is used in the sense 'to compensate for'.

♠ A x x x   ♡ A x x   ◇ A x x   ♣ A x x (6 losers : 8 minus 2)

♠ K x x x   ♡ K x x   ◇ K x x   ♣ K x x (8 losers : standard)

♠ Q x x x   ♡ Q x x   ◇ Q x x   ♣ Q x x (10 losers : 8 plus 2)

This adjustment still yields an imperfect valuation method, but it greatly improves the **LTC** . . ."

The first two of Harrison-Gray's exceptions do not add significantly to the value of an unsupported queen. Because a suit is the proposed trump suit does not give the queen enhanced powers. A trump suit with Q-x-x-x-x opposite x-x-x has little chance of avoiding three losers. The trump suit criterion only makes sense if partner can be expected to hold high card values opposite the queen. The same goes for (b) : just because partner has bid the suit the trick-taking capacity of the queen is not enhanced unless partner is likely to have high cards in the suit bid. With no suit quality requirements for opening the bidding or for responding, this basis for upgrading the queen is also risky. When the queen is supported by another honour, such as the jack in (c), the trick-taking capacity of the *combined* holding increases. The value of combined honour holdings and the value of the queen in such holdings were illustrated on pages 16-17 and 22-23 (which are worth re-reading now).

There is something not quite right in the concept of an ace balancing a queen. It does reflect the general undervaluation of aces but there is no reason why the queen should be the beneficiary. More important than the concept of balancing aces against queens are the notions of excess controls (see page 138) and of honours being more valuable when in conjunction than when split. For example, the balancing principle does not distinguish –

     ♠ A Q 5   and   ♠ A 6 5
     ♡ 6 4 2   ♡ Q 4 2

Yet the first combination is significantly more valuable than the second. If partner has no high cards in these suits, A-Q-x still has a 50% chance of two tricks while A-x-x/Q-x-x has only a 25% chance of two tricks. Give partner the ♠ K and the first combination has three tricks and the second is worth only $2\frac{1}{4}$.

Robert D. Sundby in *Bridge in the '80s* also rejects the balancing act, even though there is a contradiction between the opening and closing sentences in this extract :

"● Every unguarded queen must be counted as a loser unless it is in a suit bid or supported by partner. (Courtenay permitted an unguarded queen third or longer to be counted as only two losers if 'balanced' by an ace. I do not find any logic in the 'balancing' principle; Courtenay asks us to accept the principle on faith. I do not – I count the unguarded queen third or longer as three losers unless the suit is bid or supported. However, I recognize the queen as a plus factor. For purposes of computing the losing-trick count, let's count the queen third or longer as $2\frac{1}{2}$ losers, bearing in mind, however, that is an optimistic evaluation.)"

Conclusion : Count the queen as a winner if it has any supporting honour. With no supporting honour, count the queen as half a winner. For further clarification, see pages 16-17 and 22-23.

(3) Secondary honour combinations

(a) The A-J-10

Harrison-Gray: "Count one loser only in a suit headed by A-J-10."

Sundby: "Honour cards in combination reduce the losing-trick count. For example, the combination A-J-10 may be counted as one loser if adequate entries exist to take two finesses."

Both of these statements are astonishing in that they fail to warn of the danger of duplication and overvaluation in making such an optimistic assessment. Certainly, A-J-10 is an excellent combination when partner has three or more rags opposite (and, as Sundby points out, enough entries for two finesses) and in such a case there is a 75% chance of producing two tricks and counting just one loser is definitely a sound valuation *in that case*. However, there are many more combinations that will cause havoc to your valuation if you deduct a loser for A-J-10. What if partner has K-Q-x? Suddenly, you are overvaluing the combined potential by a full trick. What if partner has K-x-x? You are assessing the combined potential as no losers whereas there is a 50% chance of a loser. What if partner has a doubleton? The double finesse may be unwarranted. What if partner has K-x? Partner may not need or want to take the finesse. There is something very wrong in counting K-x-x opposite A-J-10 to be just as good as K-x-x opposite A-Q-x. And what if partner has a singleton opposite A-J-10? Hardly as good as a singleton opposite A-K-x, is it? A suit headed by A-J-10 will often be worth more than if headed by just A-x-x, if for no other reason than as a safeguard against bad breaks, but the value of the holding is highly dependent on what partner has in the suit. To deduct a whole loser for A-J-10 may well cause you to overvalue the partnership's potential by one trick.

Conclusion : Count A-J-10 as two losers unless you have evidence that partner has length but no high cards opposite. Count it as a plus value up to a maximum of half a trick when having to make a borderline decision.

(b) A-J-x and K-J-x holdings

Similar considerations apply to these holdings as to A-J-10. It is often better to hold A-J-x than A-x-x, but it depends on partner's holding. Opposite a singleton or rag doubleton, the jack has almost no trick-taking potential, but opposite K-x-x, it provides a 50% chance of an extra trick, while with A-J-x opposite K-10-x-x there is a certain third winner and the possibility of four tricks. A-J-x opposite Q-x-x boosts the $2\frac{1}{2}$ losers for the queen by half a trick since there are now two certain winners, while A-x-x opposite Q-x-x is only a 50% chance of two winners. On the other hand if partner has K-Q-x, the jack in A-J-x adds nothing to the playing strength.

Similar considerations apply to the K-J-x holding. It may be wasted if partner has A-Q-x, but with A-x-x opposite it adds a 50% chance of a third trick, while Q-x-x opposite it guarantees two tricks, whereas K-x-x opposite Q-x-x is very rarely two tricks if the opponents do not lead the ace.

Conclusion : Count A-J-x and K-J-x as two losers, but consider the jack with a higher honour as a plus value if you have to make a close decision.

(c) A-K-J and A-Q-J

The more honour cards in combination, the stronger the holding. If partner has no high card in the suit and has three or more cards, the jack in A-K-J adds a 50% chance of an extra trick, while the jack in A-Q-J adds a full trick : it changes a 50% chance of a second trick into a certainty and provides a 50% chance of three tricks (assuming partner has the required entries). The jack is wasted if partner has three cards with the missing honour and may be wasted if partner has a shortage in the suit. On the other hand, if partner has four or more cards with the missing honour, the jack reduces or eliminates the risk of a loser through bad breaks. A-Q-J opposite K-x-x-x-x is far superior to A-Q-x opposite K-x-x-x-x.

Similarly the 10 in combination with two or three higher honours may add significantly to the value of the hand. The ten in A-Q-10 may be wasted but it may increase your chances of an extra trick. A-K-J-10 may be worth more than A-K-J-x (it is not if partner has the queen), since if you have x-x-x opposite, the former guarantees three winners and may have four (50%), while the chance of three tricks with the latter is 70% and the chance of four tricks is only 18%. 10-9 combinations may also be an added value by providing the opportunity for secondary finesses.

Conclusion : You should tend to upgrade all hands which have the jack in combination with two higher honours or the ten in combination with two or three higher honours. Consider these as plus values when faced with a borderline decision.

(d) Q-x as two losers

While this is counted as two losers because both the ace and king are missing, the queen can certainly be a useful card. In many instances Q-x will be much more useful than x-x. Opposite A-K-x it provides an extra winner; opposite A-J-x it provides a second trick and thus may cover a loser; opposite K-x-x it provides the certainty of a trick instead of just a 50-50 chance. On the other hand, it may be useless opposite worthless holdings. The more strength partner reveals in this suit, the more useful Q-x is likely to be.

Conclusion : Count Q-x as two losers but consider it a plus value in a close decision. If partner's bidding reveals great strength in this suit, count it as a full winner. Q-x will operate as a cover card if partner has shown a strong single-suiter in the Q-x suit or if partner has shown a freak two-suiter (5-5 or 6-5 or similar) and Q-x is in one of the long suits.

(e) Other holdings

In like fashion, we count a loser for a singleton king or queen, but they might be useful opposite a strong suit. The singleton king, for example, would count as a cover card if partner pre-empted in that suit.

We count no extra tricks for J-x-x or the 10 in honour combinations like K-10-x or J-10-x, yet these minor honours may either reduce the total losers (if you had A-Q-x-x-x, would you rather have x-x-x opposite or J-10-x?) or act as a safeguard against bad breaks. Do not deduct any losers for these holdings when calculating the initial loser count after a trump fit has appeared, but when you have to make the decision to invite a game or accept a game invitation or try for a slam or not, if your hand has lots of plus values, you would be enthusiastic to push on, while if you had just the bare count as promised, you would be reluctant to venture further.

General approach : Until you know enough about partner's hand to gauge the value of secondary honour combinations accurately, do not deduct losers for them. However, until the value of your holding is clearcut, you can estimate that three plus values should be worth an extra trick.

(4) Quality of the trump support

The usefulness of the **LTC** comes into play only when a trump fit comes to light (or after partner has revealed a self-sufficient suit). The degree of fit in the trump suit is a relevant consideration when calculating the combined loser count. When you first start using the **LTC**, use the raw count whether you have located an 8-card trump fit, a 9-card trump fit, a 10-card trump fit or better. Take note of what happens with the losers expected in each case. After some experience, you will note that the raw **LTC** operates most efficiently when you have a 9-card trump fit. The following suggestions will make your **LTC** calculations more accurate :

You have a 9-card trump fit (5-4 or 6-3) : Apply the normal **LTC**.

You have a 9-card trump fit (7-2 or 8-1) : The short trump hand should assess the combined potential by estimating partner's losers and using cover cards in hand. With doubleton support and either a void or singleton outside, you may count the shortage as a *potential* cover card, but such fragile support can be easily eliminated (if they lead trumps) and the potential ruff may evaporate.

You have an 8-card trump fit : Basically, add a loser.

The 8-card trump fit is adequate but suffers from potential bad breaks. Almost one time in three you suffer a 4-1 or 5-0 break and this cuts down on the accuracy of the **LTC**, whereas with a 9-card suit, you suffer a 4-0 break only one time in ten. The effect of the number of cards in your trump suit can be seen from these combinations :

Declarer	7 5 3	8 7 5 3	9 8 7 5 3
Dummy	K Q 6 4 2	K Q 6 4 2	K Q 6 4 2
1 loser only	34%	66%	89%

The loser deducted for a poor fit may be regained if there is a significant positive factor, such as :

4-4 fit and a ruffing value : Use the normal **LTC** count. Do not deduct.

5-3 fit with better 3-card support then expected : Use the normal **LTC** count and do not deduct a loser when the 3-card trump holding has a plus value, such as J-10-x (rather than 9-x-x) or K-J-x (rather than K-x-x).

5-3 fit or 6-2 fit plus a singleton or void : Use the normal **LTC** and do not deduct a loser. The short trump holding is likely to pull its weight.

♠ 8 5 3	♠ A Q 9 6 4	♠ J 10 5	♠ A Q 9 6 4
♡ A 3	♡ K 7 4 2	♡ A 3	♡ K 7 4 2
◇ A 9 6 4 3	◇ 8	◇ A 9 6 4 3	◇ 8
♣ A 8 6	♣ 7 4 3	♣ A 8 6	♣ 7 4 3

WEST	EAST	WEST	EAST
1◇	1♠	1◇	1♠
1NT	2♡	1NT	2♡
2♠	3♣ (1)	2♠	3♣
3♠ (2)	Pass	4♠ (1)	Pass

(1) Long suit trial bid. Worth a try for game despite the 5-3 fit
(2) Not good enough in any way

(1) Because of the stronger spade holding. 4♠ is an excellent chance here, but dreadful on the other set

You have a 10-card or better fit : Basically, deduct a loser.

Such an excellent combined holding is known as a "super-fit" because the 10-card or better trump fit has exceptional potential, both within the trump suit itself (A-x-x-x-x opposite K-x-x-x-x will have no loser almost 80% of the time) and with the great potential for ruffing in both hands. If you become aware of a 10-card fit but you have no ruffing potential, use the normal LTC. Absence of ruffing potential will occur when you have 4-card support for a 6-card suit, but your hand pattern is 4-3-3-3, or when you can diagnose that both you and partner have shortages in the same suit, the phenomenon of "mirror-shapes" or extreme duplication. For examples :

OPENER	Responder A	Responder B	Responder C	Responder D
♠ A 8 7 4 2	♠ K Q 9 6 3	♠ K Q 9 6 3	♠ K Q 9 6 3	♠ K Q 9 6 3
♡ 7 5	♡ J 8 2	♡ J 8	♡ J 8 2	♡ J
◇ K Q 6	◇ A 5 3	◇ A 5 3	◇ A 5 3 2	◇ A 5 3 2
♣ J 9 3	♣ 8 4	♣ 8 4 2	♣ 8	♣ 8 4 2
8 losers	8 losers	8 losers	7 losers	7 losers

Responders A and B each have 8 losers. Deducting one loser for super-fit, you would expect to make nine tricks opposite opener's 8 losers. This is so opposite Responder A, but fails to eventuate opposite Responder B, as there is no ruffing value. With exactly the same pattern ("mirrors"), the duplication of the shortage in hearts reduces the value of the hands. Responders C and D have 7 losers and deducting a loser for super-fit, you can expect to make 10 tricks opposite 8 losers. This holds for Responder C, but not for Responder D, where responder's singleton is opposite a shortage in opener's hand, again causing duplication.

Up to game level, take the risk of such duplication and deduct a loser for super-fit, since you are covered most of the time by the likelihood that partner will have length opposite your shortage and shortage opposite your length. Accept the losses of mirror hands and duplication of shortages since they are less common than the partnership's having useful short suits when an excellent trump fit exists.

In the slam zone, however, it does not pay to be so cavalier and top pairs using the best methods can diagnose the presence of shortage duplication (for which splinter bids are an excellent aid) and mirror hands (for which modern systems using relays to determine partner's exact shape are ideal).

WEST A	EAST A	WEST B	EAST B
♠ A 8 7 4 2	♠ K Q 9 5 3	♠ A 8 7 4 2	♠ K Q 9 5 3
♡ A 5	♡ K 4 2	♡ A 5	♡ K 4
◇ A 7 6	◇ K 2	◇ A 7 6	◇ K 4 2
♣ K Q 2	♣ A J 2	♣ K Q 2	♣ A J 5

What a feeling of triumph and accomplishment if you and partner have the system and technique to be able to locate the laydown 7♠ on Set A and to avoid the hopeless grand slam on Set B. It is just as vital to avoid the hopeless slams as to bid the ones that are laydown.

(5) Adjustment for Controls

Aces and kings are the control cards. Given the same high card strength, hands which have plenty of controls are worth more than hands which have few controls. Aces are certain cover cards and kings are probable cover cards and promote the value of lesser honours in partner's hand. We count the ace as two controls and the king as one (A = 2, K = 1) and thus each suit has 3 controls and the pack contains 12 controls. As there are 40 HCP and 12 controls, the value of a control is $3\frac{1}{3}$ points. The power of extra controls is so great that they can increase the value of a hand by one or two tricks. In other words, extra controls can eliminate losers. For example :

WEST	EAST
♠ A K 8 4	♠ Q J 7 6 2
♡ A K 5 4 3	♡ 8 2
◇ 7 6	◇ A 5 4
♣ 4 3	♣ 6 5 2
6 raw losers	9 raw losers

4♠ is an excellent contract but very tough to reach. Many pairs would languish in 2♠. West is control rich but if West held ♠ K843 ♡ KQJ43 ◇ KQ ♣ 43, same points, same shape, same raw losers and 4♠ is off on top.

OPENER	Responder A	Responder B	Responder C
♠ A K 9 3	♠ 8 7 6 4 2	♠ Q J 10 7 4	♠ Q J 10 7 4
♡ A K 4	♡ 9 8 3	♡ 9 8 3	♡ 9 8
◇ A K 10 9 7	◇ 5 4	◇ 5 4	◇ 3 2
♣ 2	♣ 7 6 4	♣ 7 6 4	♣ 8 7 6 4
4 raw losers	11 losers	10 losers	9 losers

On the basis of the raw **LTC**, you would expect Responder A to produce only 9 tricks, yet 4♠ is an excellent game which we would all want to reach. A comfortable line of play might go : ruff the second club lead, play ♠ A-K, ruff a diamond, come to hand, ruff a diamond, come to hand and discard a heart loser on the (almost surely) established diamond winner, and ruff the heart loser. If spades are 3-1 and diamonds no worse than 4-2, you will make 11 tricks, while if spades are 2-2 and diamonds not 5-1, you can make 12 tricks. Similarly opposite Responder B you would expect just 10 tricks, but a small slam is a good chance, while opposite Responder C, 6♠ has excellent prospects, although the **LTC** suggests that the limit is 11 tricks. (Responder C was discussed in Chapter 6 at page 73.)

To appreciate the impact of the controls in the above Opener, put this hand (also 21 points) opposite Responder A :

♠ A Q J 9   ♡ A Q J   ◇ A Q J 10 7   ♣ 2

and see what a struggle 4♠ could be. Try this hand opposite B and C :

♠ A 9 3 2   ♡ A K 5   ◇ A Q J 10 7   ♣ K

and you would not want to be higher than 4♠. Thoughts of slam belong to the realm of fantasy and super-optimists.

HOW TO CALCULATE THE CONTROL VALUE OF YOUR HAND

Count your controls (A = 2, K = 1).

Multiply your controls by $3\frac{1}{3}$.

Count your high card points.

Subtract the high card points from the control points (controls $\times 3\frac{1}{3}$).

If the answer is positive, you have control excess. If the answer is negative, you have control deficiency. If the difference is very small, do not make any adjustment, but if the answer is 2 or more, you should make an appropriate adjustment, slightly conservatively, as follows :

+2 or more : Deduct half a loser

+6 or more : Deduct a loser

+9 or more : Deduct $1\frac{1}{2}$ losers

–2 or more : Add half a loser

–6 or more : Add a loser

Consider the opening hand in the previous example :

♠ A K 9 3   ♡ A K 4   ◇ A K 10 9 7   ♣ 2

The hand has 21 HCP and 4 raw losers. It contains 9 controls, which is equivalent to 30 control points ($9 \times 3\frac{1}{3}$). $30 - 21 = 9$. Deduct $1\frac{1}{2}$ losers from the raw loser count of 4 and you have a realistic value of $2\frac{1}{2}$ losers, thus warranting *a force to game* on those values.

Another way to look at the same phenomenon is to consider an average hand of 10 HCP which contains an ace, a king, a queen and a jack, which includes 3 controls. For every 10 HCP you hold, your hand should contain 3 controls. Thus, if you hold 20 HCP, the control expectancy is 6. The hand above with 9 controls has the control expectancy of a 30-point hand, yet it has only 21 HCP. Thus it is very "control rich" and this can be translated into trick-taking capacity (or playing strength).

If you want to adjust control excess or deficiency into points, a fair guide is to subtract your high card points from your control points and divide the answer by 5. Add or subtract this from your high card total to derive your control-adjusted total. On this basis, the above example hand with 21 HCP would be adjusted to around 23 points. No wonder it is too strong for an opening bid of one. Here is another example :

♠ A K 4 3   This hand contains 18 HCP and many players
♡ A 9   using a 16-18 1NT opening would indeed open
◇ A K 6   it 1NT. However, the hand contains 8 controls
♣ 8 7 4 3   which is $26\frac{2}{3}$ control points, $8\frac{2}{3}$ points more
             than the HCP. It is thus worth about $1\frac{1}{2}$
points more than the HCP and is too strong for a 16-18 1NT opening. Similar control adjustments will assist you in assessing your hand as minimum or maximum for the range shown.

Most standard texts reflect the value of controls when they recommend that you add 1 point for holding all four aces and deduct 1 point for an aceless hand. This is only a rough guide and comparing your controls with expectancy will give you a more accurate guide. This table of controls expected for high card point values will assist you :

HCP	Controls expected	HCP	Controls expected	HCP	Controls expected
0	0	12	4	24	7
1	0	13˙	4	25	8
2	0	14	4	26	8
3	1	15	5	27	8
4	1	16	5	28	8
5	1	17	5	29	9
6	2	18	5	30	9
7	2	19	6	31	9
8	2	20	6	32	10
9	3	21	6	33	10
10	3	22	7	34	10
11	3	23	7	35	10

Using the adjustments for controls will remove this apparent paradox :

$$\spadesuit \text{ A 7 4} \qquad \heartsuit \text{ A 5 2} \qquad \diamondsuit \text{ A 8 4} \qquad \clubsuit \text{ A 6 3 2}$$

Superficially, this has 8 losers and is worse than the 7 losers expected for a normal opening. However, the hand has 8 controls, $26\frac{2}{3}$ control points. The difference is $10\frac{2}{3}$, making a difference of almost 2 losers, so that this hand should be assessed not as 8 losers but as 6-$6\frac{1}{2}$ losers, just as you would expect from a hand around 16 points.

Control-rich hands can make a grand slam child's play while lesser holdings make a grand slam a poor prospect or a foolish gamble.

OPENER	Responder A	Responder B	Responder C
♠ A K 8 6 4	♠ Q 9 7 5 3	♠ Q 9 7 5 3	♠ Q 9 7 5 3
♡ A 7	♡ K 5 4	♡ K J 4	♡ K Q J
◇ A 4	◇ K 7 3	◇ K 7 3	◇ K 7 3
♣ 8 6 4 2	♣ A K	♣ A Q	♣ A 3

Opposite Responder A, a grand slam in spades is there for the taking. Opposite Responder B, the chance of 7♠ is only 50%, the club finesse, not worth the risk and 6 ♠ is high enough. Opposite Responder C, there is no chance for 7 ♠ and yet all three hands have the same high card total. The challenge you and partner face in the bidding is to be able to judge such hands accurately and reach the excellent slams, avoid the poor ones and know what you are doing. It is no credit to you if you find the right spot by sheer luck, although the result may be profitable.

Conclusion

You now have enough information to apply the **LTC**, starting with just the raw count and applying the recommended adjustments in Chapter 10 as you gain more experience and more confidence. If you consider the **LTC** as a useful adjunct to your normal bidding methods, it will be a valuable tool, indeed. If you look on it as a panacea for all bidding problems, you will be bitterly disappointed and may reject the **LTC**, thus losing the many benefits it provides. The **LTC** has a limited application, to hands where a trump fit exists or one player has a long, self-sufficient suit. Within that context, it is an excellent valuation technique. It is not infallible but you will find it is more accurate than any point count methods.

One of the great advantages of the **LTC** is that you can use it even if your partner has never heard of it. It is not a convention or a matter for partnership agreement (unless bids are defined in terms of losers). As long as you can estimate partner's point count, you can assess partner's losers. The more you know about the shape of partner's hand, the more accurate will be your assessment of partner's losers. These tables will help :

Partner's points	Losers expected	Cover cards expected	Partner's pattern	Maximum losers
0-6	10-12	0-1	4-3-3-3	12
7-9	8-9	1-2	4-4-3-2	11
10-12	7-8	2-3	5-3-3-2	11
13-15	6-7	3-4	4-4-4-1	10
16-18	5-6	4-5	5-4-4-0	9
19-21	4-5	5-6	5-4s/6-3s	10
22-24	3-4	6-7	5-5s/6-4s	9
25-27	2-3	7-8	6-5s	8

If you know a fair bit about partner's shape and points, you can deduct the cover cards expected from the maximum losers for that shape and calculate the number of losers partner should have.

Good luck and happy bridging. May this be the start of more accurate, more profitable and more pleasant bridge for you.